Attitude Therapy

Deb Copeland

Bloomington, IN Milton Keynes, UK

authorHOUSE®

AuthorHouse™
1663 Liberty Drive, Suite 200
Bloomington, IN 47403
www.authorhouse.com
Phone: 1-800-839-8640

AuthorHouse™ UK Ltd.
500 Avebury Boulevard
Central Milton Keynes, MK9 2BE
www.authorhouse.co.uk
Phone: 08001974150

First published by AuthorHouse 8/23/2006

ISBN: 1-4259-5790-0 (sc)

Library of Congress Control Number: 2006907561

Printed in the United States of America
Bloomington, Indiana

This book is printed on acid-free paper.

Front Cover Photo by Rick Lee
Back Cover Photo by Michael Switzer
Cover by John Auge
Editor Dianne Schilling

To Don Lucci …

… who has been a mother and father to me,
my best friend, confidant, caregiver, boyfriend, lover,
father of my children, husband and soul mate …
who allows me space enough to grow and heal
but keeps me close enough that I always feel secure.

Acknowledgments

My deepest thanks to Matt, Erica and Ryan for their love, encouragement, criticism and compliments, and to Molly, Tate, Maggie and Morgan for putting up with my stress during this project. Maggie, you kept me motivated to finish with that cleverest of guilt trips: "Mommy, I can't wait until the book is finished so you can be a mommy again."

Thank you to Beth Daniels, my best friend and a constant source of inspiration, and to all those friends whom I ignored or abandoned in mid-sentence when my eyes glazed over with ideas for the book, including my tennis team, running buddies, church family and prayer group.

Endless thanks to the many friends who carried me through my illness and hospital stays by cooking, cleaning, babysitting, driving and oh, yes, caroling (though the talent was questionable). Bless you Brent and Fran, Martha and Kim for helping me to rear my children by attending sports competitions, church plays, piano recitals, musicals and numerous other functions. Thank you Carol, Joan and Jean for babysitting, cooking ,cleaning and ironing, and for your Christian influence on my children, and Kamilla, my driver for the nine-months during which I was not allowed to drive, whose job was fondly dubbed, "Driving Ms. Crazy."

Special recognition to Aunt Mary, Aunt Freda, and Tina for helping me tend to my ailing mother, and to Marie, Virginia and Maxine for filling in as second mothers after she was gone. (I was so bad it took three.) To friends who played significant roles while I was growing up and tried to fill the void: Brownie, Neva, Belinda, Polly, Kerry, Steve, Marti, Shari, Diane, Francis and Nora. And to my friend, Laura, who is like a sister.

Thanks to Dr. Ayoubi and Dr. Hoylman for helping me to launch my career and study for the PA boards. To my medical cronies, Joan, Theresa and Debi. And to my business advisors Norman Daniels, George Patterson, Bill McKee, Rob Berthold, Rick Whisner and Dick Williams.

A special thank you to my girlfriend, physician and "manuscript coach," Dr. Kathleen Mimnagh, and to Randall J. Hill, M.D. and Dr. Donna Slayton for your love, compassion and encouragement down through the years.

Thanks to Pam Moll and Diane Tate for your tireless efforts to read my scribbling on paper napkins, parking tickets, the backs of my children's school papers and report cards, church bulletins and wherever else I deposited a thought or story, including dictated tapes with car pool, soccer and swim-practice noises in the background. Whether I wrote in traffic, on planes, in restaurants, movies or waiting lines; whether in daylight or waking in the dark, your skill at deciphering my efforts was awesome.

Thank you to Linda Kelly, Kim Brown, Greg White, Marsha Boggess, Jeff Fetty, Lalena Price, Scot Jackson, Jim Wilkerson and John Auge, for giving completely of your artistic abilities, time and talents to help me reach my dream.

Deepest appreciation to my research and development team: Mary Jane Ayoob, Gretchen Murphy, Lesli Forbes and Sara Ryan, who worked tirelessly around the clock, proofing, reading, editing, marketing and securing media coverage. And thank you to those who gave selflessly of your friendship and talents proofing the manuscript from it's conception.

Thanks to Skip Makely for educating me in the art and science of publishing a book, along with authors Wendy Enelow and Barbara Levine. And to my publisher, AuthorHouse.

Finally, to the many heroes whose stories of survival fill this book: thank you for granting me the privilege of interviewing you.

And to my editor, Dianne Schilling—God bless you!

You have brains in your head; you have feet in your shoes.
You can steer yourself in any direction you choose.
You're on your own and you know what you know.
You're the guy who'll decide where to go!

—Theodore Suess Geisel
The Cat in the Hat

Table of Contents

Introduction

Attitude Begins with Me

My name is Deb Copeland and I am a survivor. I am also an educator, entrepreneur, philanthropist, author, wife and mother. More than 20 years ago, I created a course called Attitude Therapy, which I have taught to thousands of people in the workplace. I tell my students that attitude is not about what happens to them, but, rather, about how they *respond* to what happens. I encourage people to have a plan ready *before* disaster strikes. Tragedy is guaranteed to come into our lives in one form or another, so it makes sense to develop an attitude of survival before it does. I speak from experience, because tragedy has visited me multiple times. My goal is to have people learn from my life and take charge of their own.

A Happy Childhood

I grew up in South Charleston, West Virginia, with a two-year stint in Bend, Oregon, during the second and third-grades. We were a very happy family. We had our ups and downs, but plugged along in what seemed to me the perfect "Ozzie and Harriet" existence. My parents appeared to be extremely compatible and content in each other's company. They enjoyed planning meals and cooking together. When Mother washed dishes, Dad would be right there with a dish towel over his shoulder, drying, whistling, and singing. We visited my maternal grandmother almost every weekend, and unlike many men, Dad adored his mother-in-law.

My father was a very happy, positive individual, while Mother was more serious. She had a sense of humor, but a no-nonsense attitude about manners and doing things properly. Dad was the balancing force. He liked to cut up, sing, talk and have lots of fun. My sister, Jackie, four years older than I, was pretty much the straight-laced, follow-the-rules-and-don't-test-the-waters type of kid, and a straight-A student.

In the early years, I was involved in majorettes, tennis, tap, ballet and jazz dancing. I ran track and briefly tossed a basketball (all those hands and arms in my face got to be a real problem) and did some cheerleading. My grades were average or slightly below. I had the ability to excel academically, but was too busy having fun to develop those resources until later in life.

When I was 14, my parents announced that Dad was getting a job transfer and would be commuting to and from Pennsylvania for a while. Jackie and I were told that the traveling would be short-term. Either the family would move, or Dad would come back. We would see how things went and go from there.

After a time, Jackie and I began to suspect that the family was never going to reunite. We couldn't pinpoint the problem, but sensed that something was amiss and began to ask, "Where's Dad? When is he coming back? Why haven't we heard from him?" We told Mom that we wouldn't mind relocating if it would make her happier. (In reality, my sister was totally against moving. She was older than I and had a boyfriend. Leaving would have destroyed her.)

Divorce and a Dreaded Disease

Mother sat my sister and me down one day and said she needed to be honest with us. I could tell by her expression that this talk was going to be more serious than I could handle. Her face was pale and full of anguish. I can still feel the quiet in the room. She told us that she had terminal cancer. For once in my life I was speechless. The room swirled and I felt like throwing up. With a lump in my throat, I managed to blurt out, "Where's

Dad?" then quickly remembered that he was in Pennsylvania. Only a few minutes before, in the same room, my mother had given us the news that Dad was leaving permanently. He had found another woman and planned to live with her. That news had left me devastated. Now I felt completely destroyed. Slowly, the three of us knelt by the sofa and prayed.

Years later, working as a physician-assistant, I encountered many people who could not bear to be around loved ones when they were gravely ill. They were there for the good times, but couldn't cope with the emotional trauma of seeing someone they cared for suffer. I am not sure if that was my father's problem. He'd had a number of affairs, so maybe the real instigator was a mid-life crisis. At any rate, he chose a different life for himself. To this day, I am not sure why. On the few occasions that I have attempted to discuss it with Dad, the entire subject caused him such pain, I dropped it.

I have never really come to grips with the family breakup. In terms of the big picture, it probably doesn't matter, but to me personally it does. I believe that all of the things that happen to us in childhood happen for a reason, and we learn from them, whether we realize it at the time or not.

Fortunately, my mother, in her wisdom, decided not to be small, mean, and ugly about the divorce. If I had been in her place, I doubt that I could have handled the situation as well. Mom told my sister and me that, regardless of what the marriage had become, Dad was our father and we must not feel bitter toward him. She urged us to pursue individual relationships with him and stressed that the only part of the family constellation that was broken was their marriage. She forgave him and remained on friendly terms with him to make sure that we had what we needed in life. Neither her tone nor her words ever strayed from that message. I never heard her say an unkind word about him.

Distressed people sometimes reach a point where they deliberately tear down the emotional well-being of others, inventing problems and issues that don't even exist. When a divorced parent talks about his or her former spouse in an extremely negative way, instability is created in the lives of the children. Many a young person's life has been ruined by such destructive behavior. It is morally wrong to tear down the relationships of others.

I was fortunate to have a mother with inordinate class, pride, and dignity. Rather than drag Jackie and me through an emotional hell, she focused on helping us build good relationships with our father. What really sticks in my mind is that, throughout this time, Mom had cancer. She was dying while helping us cope with the divorce in a positive way. She wanted to preserve the closeness between Dad and us for when we needed him, after she passed away. It is painful to think back and imagine what was on her mind. I just can't fathom a person being so kind.

Caring for Mom

My mother—best friend, mentor and cheerleader—fought a respectable fight and succumbed three years later. In recalling the details of my mother's illness, I remember certain things, but not in any real order. I remember sitting by her bed watching the urine turn from yellow, to brown, to blood, and then stop altogether as her kidneys shut down. I remember helping with her colostomy—running soapy water into the tubes to irrigate it. Looking back, I can only imagine how difficult and humiliating it must have been to lie there and watch a 15-year-old care for her as though she were a child. I remember her mouth and tongue turning black a couple of days prior to her passing. I remember sitting hour upon hour with one of my aunts beside her bed waiting for that final moment—watching as systems closed down. Those scars are still with me.

I skipped school every day to be with my mother in the hospital. That was my sophomore-going-on-junior year. I had obtained permission for my absences and arranged special testing to compensate for the missed work.

During the final months, Mother was in a great deal of pain. The nurses at the hospital taught me to administer her pain medication by hypodermic. They had me practice by injecting oranges. It was one of the most difficult tasks I've ever done. I was just 15, my son Ryan's age now, performing as a mature, responsible adult and caregiver. She was so thin at that point, her buttocks were practically nonexistent. I would lie awake at night and listen to her groan, crying and praying that either she or I would fall asleep so that I wouldn't have to give her another injection.

When I gave her a shot, she would cry out that I was killing her. She complained that I wanted to hurt her and that I was rough. It was terribly depressing to watch her disintegrate before my eyes.

We had no money that year at Christmas, so my mother wrapped up a broach that had been my grandmother's and presented it to me as my gift. We were alone and the moment was bittersweet. At 15, I wanted things like the other kids had, but felt too hurt to say anything.

I was the one who took my mom to visit her physician, Dr. Dawson, so he was accustomed to dealing only with me. Even though I was young, he looked straight into my eyes when he talked to me, never holding back the truth, yet always offering hope.

Once I asked him, "How much more time do we have?" He responded that Mom's kidneys appeared to be failing and estimated the number of hours she had left. But, he added, "I am not God and I won't play God. At any moment things could change." Dr. Dawson prided himself in never rendering time limits of any kind. He said that was God's department.

Desperation, Marriage and Work

When my mother finally died, I was devastated. I turned to alcohol and drugs and my life spiraled out of control. After three years of abusing my body, spirit, brain and soul—and the people around me—I finally started getting my act together. I went back to school, studied nursing and respiratory therapy and became a pediatric physician assistant.

The work was very fulfilling and I loved it, but I always felt a certain restlessness. Though I have a caregiver mentality, I think I chose the medical field in part to compensate for the emotional trauma of losing my mother. I've seen numerous people enter nursing school at 40, 50 or 60 after the loss of a spouse or child. When a dreaded disease claims the life of a loved one, you want to do something about it.

At 23, I married a man 15 years older than I. We had a child, Mathew, within two years. Six months into the marriage, I realized that my husband had some problems, though I wasn't sure what they were until I learned that he had made another woman pregnant. We divorced.

I had just started a job that allowed me to accept supplemental work on the side. I could do the histories and physicals for new admissions and some billing at night from my home, so it was almost like being my own temp service. But I was spread too thin. That's when I left the health care field and started a temporary employment service.

Many of the doctors with whom I worked at the hospital encouraged me. With no money, a house payment and a small child, I worked 60-hour weeks, only to discover that none of the doctors who encouraged me had any intention of hiring my workers—at least not at first. I had to prove myself.

I had started my business at a young age, when discrimination against women in the workplace was commonplace—especially women with little experience, like me. I was only 25. When I tried to recruit business, many doors were closed to me. Tirelessly, I worked to prove myself and build a reputation in the community.

Obtaining a line of credit posed another hurdle. Bankers were not overly anxious to give money to a kid, especially one who had neither financial resources nor a business education. Each Friday, I had to meet payroll. In a temporary service, you pay your employees, *then* bill your clients. The money doesn't turn around overnight, so you wait. I needed a line of credit to survive. I had to buy an insurance policy on my life so that the bank would get its money back in the event of my death. As the business grew, so did the need for larger amounts of money to sustain it.

Managing hundreds of people produced heartaches and headaches, pleasure and pain. I have seen grown men jump over the reception desk because of a mistake on their paycheck. I have received threats to my life as a result of letting people go. Looking back, it's no wonder I got sick. The stress was enough to put any sane person in a mental hospital. But I thrived on it, and the business grew and grew. I worked tirelessly from early morning until late at night. Only now, when I reflect on those times, do I recognize how demanding the business was.

Growing a Business

I had survived the loss of my mother to colon cancer, the loss of my father to divorce, the loss of my self-respect to a desperate lifestyle, the loss of my husband to another woman, and now I faced a failing business.

I was still driving a rusted out 1960 Volkswagen and wearing little skirts with knee socks. That wasn't working. I realized that to *be* successful I had to *act* successful, so I retired the youthful costume, lost the beat-up car and donned a new attitude. Though deeply in debt, I bought an expensive navy blue suit and a nice used car and proceeded to fake it until I made it. I started with one employee and grew the business to 4,000 employees servicing seven states. I did not have the knowledge. I did not have the strength. I didn't even have encouragement. But I did have the will.

I began to offer secretarial, light industrial, and retail services. Business opportunities materialized. For no reason other than respect for my hard work, the owner of another temporary agency retired and sold her business to me for $200 a month over 20 years. With the help of my assistant, colleague and friend, Billie Henning, the business grew and flourished. Then a competitor who was leaving the industry literally gave me his business—another unheard of deal resulting in more growth.

Smart Temporary Services went on to become one of the top independently owned temporary services in the U.S. and the largest in West Virginia, covering a seven-state region. Eventually, I earned not only money, but respect, recognition and multiple awards in the industry.

Puzzling Symptoms

Life was good, with lots of hard work and endless business decisions, until one morning I woke up with knees the size of Texas and lymph nodes as big as oranges. Originally, I was diagnosed with Crohn's Disease—then Lupus, Sjogrens

Syndrome, Raynaud's Phenomenon, Diabetes, Mononucleosis, Chronic Fatigue Syndrome and relapsing Polychondritis. The final diagnosis was Mixed Connective Tissue Disease. The symptoms included joint stiffness and pain, irritable bowel, dry eyes and mouth and extreme sensitivity to cold. Simply holding an ice-filled glass hurt clear to my elbow. My blood pressure was like a yo-yo, fluctuating from high to low in a matter of moments, and my blood sugar was out of control. I had migraines and seizures and a host of other problems.

There were times during those years of serial diagnoses when I lost all hope and experienced profound disappointment and despair. When a lab test failed to reveal the expected result, the diagnosis of the day would be withdrawn and other tests ordered, which in turn revealed more puzzling results and led to additional diagnostic hopscotch. The cycle of remissions and flare-ups was like a roller coaster ride. Still, amid the depression, fear and failing health, I managed to believe that everything would be all right. In retrospect, I am not sure if my optimism came from being a bull-headed control freak, or a positive attitude "wannabe." Whatever it was, it kept me going. I discovered that I could make matters much worse by complaining about my problems. I discovered that "the more you stir it, the worse it stinks." By talking obsessively about your problems they become insurmountable.

Finally, through heavy use of steroids, chemotherapy, and a host of other drugs (at one point I was taking 20 or more pills a day), I was able to get my life back to some semblance of normalcy. Oh, I forgot one thing. After experiencing a grand-mal seizure and losing consciousness on the golf course, I was diagnosed with a meningioma brain tumor. Some players will use any excuse to explain a poor score on the front nine!

Happiness and Health at Last

During this difficult time I married a wonderful man. Don is my life partner, lover and the father of our six children—his daughter, Erica, my son, Matt, our son, Ryan, and three children we later adopted. Today, Erica is my best girlfriend and running buddy. We can jog seven miles together and never run out of things to talk about.

I experienced more health complications over the next several years. The only good complication was the cesarean delivery of a beautiful baby boy, Ryan Lucci, known as "Little King" by his older brother and sister.

Getting Ryan here was not easy. I found out that I was pregnant during a very turbulent Crohn's disease flare-up. I was taking steroids and a few other drugs. There was some discussion of terminating the pregnancy. In our seven years of marriage, Don and I had already lost one child because of my health. We decided not to interrupt this pregnancy.

One day my 12-year-old son said to me, "Mom, do you believe half of the stuff you teach us? If so, there is your answer: *believe.* I was taken aback that he understood the decisions we were facing and was elated to hear his advice. Complete bed rest was prescribed during the sixth week of the pregnancy. I developed gestational diabetes, was on a terbutaline pump to prevent pre-term labor and was still taking prednisone. I was also trying to run a business. Unbeknownst to my doctors, I began to withdraw the prednisone during the pregnancy so that I could nurse Ryan upon delivery.

The pregnancy was up and down, and very risky, but we made it. We had much to be thankful for, including an immediate remission of all of my symptoms. Sometimes soft-tissue diseases are shocked into remission by the major changes of pregnancy or delivery. I experienced remission immediately after delivery. As a matter of fact, I went to work around day three with the baby in tow.

We left for a vacation in Hilton Head on the four-week anniversary of Ryan's birth. I rode a bike and jogged. I remember going in for my six-week checkup. The doctor looked as though he were seeing a ghost. When I checked out perfectly, he encouraged me to resume running. You should have seen his face when I confessed that I had been running for two weeks. I had been admitted to the hospital nine times during the pregnancy for complications. Trying to get a healthy baby delivered had been almost as stressful for him as for me. We celebrated together!

When people ask how I made it through, I credit my faith in God and positive attitude. When I learned that my mother was going to die, I refused to be defeated. I possessed a childlike resilience, an adolescent's will to survive. At no time did I consider the possibility of *not* surviving. I was unaware that there was a choice. I developed habits of persistence that have carried over to my adult life. If you don't possess an innate resilience, learn from my heartache. You too can survive!

1

Why Attitude Counts

The first reaction of many people upon hearing the story of my recovery from multiple debilitating illnesses is that perhaps I was repeatedly misdiagnosed. Their second reaction is, "She's a nut!" Their third is, "Wow, there really is something to this attitude stuff."

Attitude Therapy is the deliberate study of positive thinking. It is a preventive practice that will prepare you for real-life situations in which attitude may play a deciding role. Many inconveniences, problems and demanding experiences will arise in your lifetime. Most of these events will not march into your life in any particular order. They will just happen. When two or more occur at once, each one will demand top priority. Problems are not issued on a check-off list with instructions on how to cope. Emergencies, such as illness, depression, the loss of a child, divorce and financial crises do not wait until you are prepared and have your life in tip-top shape. They arrive without fanfare, causing chaos, frustration and reactive thinking. How you respond to these life situations to a large extent determines how happy or how miserable you are.

You may wonder how something as intangible and fleeting as attitude can make such a difference when coping with disasters and emergencies—why your thoughts and words count so much. I hope that in reading this book you find the answers to your questions. I hope that you come to agree with me that attitude is not about what happens to you, but, rather, how you respond to what happens.

Attitude Takes Practice

You have what it takes to rise above any hardship, but doing so requires concentrated effort—what I like to refer to as "time on task." You must devote appropriate time and energy to thinking differently and training yourself to believe that you can achieve positive results. The situations you face in life are often not as important as your reactions to those situations. It is hard to accept difficult circumstances, but it is important to respect each setback while honoring the lessons it teaches. If something difficult happens, you must know in advance how to recover. When you have a method, you can handle almost anything.

In the book, *The Wind Is My Mother,* Medicine Man Bear Heart shares the story of a young mother who asked him to visit her in the hospital after the birth of her child. The infant was born without arms, had webbed feet and numerous scars. Through prayer and discussion, he and the mother were able to find a blessing in the child's birth.

Bear Heart shared a story with the new mother of a similar situation in which a boy was born without arms. In the story, the doctors asked the husband to stay by his wife's side as she regained consciousness, and to tell her the news. When she awoke, the husband looked at his wife and told her they had a beautiful baby boy. "But Mary, he was born without any arms," he said sadly. Mary lay there for a moment with her eyes closed. Then she opened them and, with a beautiful smile on her face, looked up into the eyes of her husband and said, "John, God must have known how much he needed us."

According to Bear Heart, in the Muskogee Creek Indian culture, people believe that the Creator has a reason for bringing each child into the world. The woman realized that her son was put in her care for a reason, and it was her duty to make his life as comfortable as possible.

Reading and hearing stories like this is a form of Attitude Therapy practice. When we hear an exemplary story, most of us experience a degree of empathy with the people who actually lived through the experience. Our brains are wired to walk a few steps in the other person's shoes, to wonder how we would respond in similar circumstances. If we can avoid it, most of us would rather not experience tragedy in order to learn how to handle tragedy. Vicarious experiences accompanied by empathy are reasonable substitutes.

Bear Heart's book touched me deeply. It took me on a journey of self-awareness. During my early years, I hated my father for leaving me. But reading the words of Bear Heart proved to be a major life-changing experience. I totally forgave my father as a result of Bear Heart's words, which touched my very soul. You see, Bear Heart and his wife, Regina Water Spirit, are Native American Creek Indians. My father's grandmother was part Creek Indian. Many of the words of wisdom my father spoke to me as a child were passed down from his mother. It was a revelation to me that Dad had contributed to my values in a huge way and played a significant role in nurturing the attitude of survival I embrace today.

I no longer looked at my father as a criminal deserter after I recognized the positive influence he'd had on my development. Instead of focusing on what he had done *to me*, I began to cherish what he had done *for me*.

Attitude Colors Perception

Have you ever noticed that when you think things are going to go wrong, they somehow do? The rain doesn't stop because you refuse to see it or talk about it. But if you change how you respond to the rain, the weather doesn't seem so bad. You have the ability to look at things differently. How you look at a situation and how you choose to envision its ramifications play significant roles in determining the outcome.

At age 17, Ronnie was diagnosed with MS (Multiple Scleroris). The doctors shared the prognosis with her parents, but the parents decided not to pass on the news to their daughter. Ronnie's boyfriend also knew the prognosis, but he too said nothing.

Ronnie led what she believed was a typical teenager's life—not the beginning of a life of disability. When she was finally told of her illness at age 27, she was shocked and frightened. Nevertheless, she continued to live normally and even travelled in her spare time. Forty years later, although she relies on a wheelchair for mobility, Ronnie doesn't feel handicapped. She plays bridge every day and leads what she terms a "splendid life."

Ronnie's toughest decision was whether or not to have chidren. After getting pregnant, doctors urged her to abort the fetus to avoid putting a strain on her body, but she decided to follow through with the pregnancy. Ronnie's daughter has always been a tremendous source of strength to her mother, and now a granddaughter is pitching in as well. Ronnie admits that things are getting tougher as she ages, but because of her positive attitude and strong family, she lives life to the fullest. Although I don't recommend keeping patients in the dark about their conditions, perhaps Ronnie's adolescent belief that she was just like the other kids helped her to internalize a positive attitude through those formative years.

Of course, not everyone would approach MS with the same can-do attitude. Different people respond to the exact same situation differently. One spouse views a marital disagreement as an opportunity for dialogue. The other sees it as a sign that the marriage is in trouble. Two women, each with the same type and stage of breast cancer, respond to their diagnoses differently. One gives up hope, goes home, pulls the covers up over her head and prepares to die. The other rolls up her sleeves determined to fight, casts aside the doctor's prognosis and stops at nothing to live. Or consider two mothers whose children have the same illness. One gives up, becomes depressed and loses hope. The other "fakes it 'til she makes it." She gets up each day and says, "Okay, this is what we are going to do." She sets goals and makes plans and sticks with them, encouraging the child by her enthusiasm, confident body language and winning attitude.

Twelve days before her sixth birthday, Meredith Frost was diagnosed with Wilms' Tumor Stage IV. In lay terms, the child had a cancerous growth that was bursting through her kidney, enveloping surrounding organs and a major artery. The cancer had spread to both lungs, which were filled with over 100 small tumors.

Eight weeks before the diagnosis, Meredith had broken out in hives for no apparent reason. Some of the people who examined the child thought the problem involved the appendix, but the pain was on the opposite side. Meredith had been unusually lethargic and sleepy, so her mother, Stephanie, thought it might be mononucleosis.

One night in the middle of a snowstorm, when Meredith was very sick, Stephanie asked a friend who was a nurse to come over. Examining the sick child, the friend felt the tumor and had Stephanie feel it, too. It was the size of a grapefruit.

Doctors speculated that Meredith had been born with the tumor. It had grown very slowly, like a ball in her kidney, with many smaller balls in her lungs. Early in the treatment process, Meredith was depressed, weak, tired and sick from the chemotherapy and needles. She would say, "Why me? Why can't I just play? Why do I have this bad ball in my belly?"

Stephanie was devastated by the prognosis. "You hear the words coming from the doctors and suddenly find yourself praying for things you never dreamed would matter to you, such as a favorable histology of the cancer cells, and a 50 percent chance of survival. Overnight your life is like that of a character on 'ER.'" Stephanie used to watch the parents in those episodes with empathy and despair, wondering how they did it.

When the doctor described Meredith's cancer and suggested a combination of surgery, chemotherapy and radiation, Stephanie felt helpless. "For the first time, I couldn't fix or even help my child feel better," she said. "But I could do one thing: I could think positive thoughts and have positive intentions, and perhaps that would help her heal."

From that point on, Stephanie disciplined herself to be positive about her daughter's cancer. "I told her she was going to beat the bad ball in her belly," she explained. "I told her how strong she was, how great she was doing through *every* stage of her treatment. I told her that she was going to be a *Cancer Star.*"

At school, Meredith's teacher took the same approach. Instead of Meredith being the sick girl whose hair was falling out, the kindergarten class made her their star and rallied behind her. They made greeting cards, a book, and, with the help of a friend's mom, a quilt. They even put together a basket filled with hats that they brought from home. Whenever Meredith came to school, they would all don their hats so that she wouldn't be the only one whose head was covered.

Each night before Meredith went to bed, Stephanie would say the prayer, "Now I Lay Me Down to Sleep" with her daughter. But they would add another wish at the end:

Dear God:
Please make me see that you are always around me,
holding my hand and kissing my forehead. Whenever
I am hurt and whenever I cry, I know that you love me
no matter what. Thank you God.
Amen.

After prayers, Stephanie and Meredith often played a visualization game. Meredith would pick a character from *Winnie the Pooh* (for example, Piglet) to travel through her body with Christopher Robbin. She pretended that her body was the Enchanted Forest. They would walk hand-in-hand, beginning in her lungs and ending at the big ball in her kidney. As they walked they would stomp on all the bad balls. Meredith imagined they were zapping them away.

Within six months, Meredith was through her protocol, the fastest patient in memory for many of the staff at Children's Hospital of Philadelphia (CHOP). Surgeons removed the large tumor, but some of the smaller lung tumors had disappeared completely by the fourth week of treatment. Today Meredith is a healthy, confident 11-year-old.

Stephanie attributes her daughter's success to three things: CHOP medical protocol; natural treatments, such as acidophilus, milk thistle and bovine cartridge, which her doctors allowed; and a positive attitude practiced each and every day.

Attitude Imparts Purpose

In his book, *Personhood*, Leo Buscaglia writes that when an individual fully functions as a person, death is not a threat. Instead, it serves as life's greatest ally, compelling us to live life now, in the moment. "It (death) tells us that it is not the quantity of our days, or hours, or years that matter, but rather the quality of the time spent," he writes. "Every day is new. Every moment is fresh."

A sense of purpose and hope can do wonders for your health and well-being. Often doctors are unaware of the need for meaning in life. As a result, they fail to understand dramatic improvements in the conditions of their patients.

Dr. Bernie S. Siegel, who specializes in self-healing, writes in the book, *Peace, Love & Healing,* about a letter he received from another physician concerning a woman both had treated. The patient, who had extensive breast cancer, had returned to the doctor's office nearly five months after he had sent her to a nursing home for end-of-life care. Seigel's colleague wrote that he had never seen her looking so well.

Siegel asked a medical student to track down the woman and learn the reason for the improvement. "The woman told the student that when she got to the nursing home, she found conditions there so unbearable and depressing that she led a revolution among the other 'inmates' to insist that they receive better treatment. She spent time talking with the staff about the tenderness and love the patients needed, and she transformed the place."

The challenge had given her a meaning in life. It had given her purpose and delight. After her transformation of the nursing home, Siegel says she was able to go home and even bought herself a new car. The woman's survival sprang from this newfound purpose.

People who cultivate positive attitudes tend to see purpose in everything they do. When they make mistakes, they don't condemn themselves or feel like failures. They look for the lesson in each mistake and try not to repeat it. They view mistakes as successive approximations, as trial and error leading to eventual success. Positive people seem to grow as human beings with each new experience, whether it is wonderful and thrilling, fearful and abhorrent, or anything in between.

The truth is, we are mortal. We have a limited number of days. We live our lives in the shadow of our own mortality. Today is a gift. We must live in the now, focusing on today. We can't worry about yesterday and we can't stress over tomorrow.

Attitude Is Infectious

What kinds of attitudes are you carrying around with you, supportive or negative? Just as you are what you eat, you are what you think.

When I walk into a room to conduct a class or give a presentation, I often start by saying, "How many of you woke up today in a fantastic, exceptional mood?" I always hear a little bit of grumbling, and a few people in the class laugh. One or two start to raise their hands, but hesitate because they don't know if I'm serious. I rephrase the question and ask, "How many of you woke up, looked out your window and immediately thought of three or four terrific things you were looking forward to today?" At this point I often hear comments like, "When I looked out it was snowing," or "When I looked out it was still dark."

My questions help most people realize that everyone has the choice to wake up with a wonderful attitude or a poor attitude. It doesn't matter what day it is, or if it's snowing outside, or raining, or sunny, or pitch black. Nearly all of us can wake up feeling relatively happy if we choose to. So I ask the question again, "How many of you woke up feeling exceptionally good?" A few people raise their hands. Then I ask, "How many of you, prior to arriving here today, complimented another person face to face, or made an *exceptionally* thoughtful comment to someone? For example, maybe you walked up to a colleague and said, "I love that dress. That is the sharpest dress I have seen in years." On the other hand, maybe you didn't see anybody before you came into this room. You sat down and the first person you really focused on was the speaker. I moseyed up to the podium, you leaned toward your friend sitting next to you and whispered, "Have you ever seen anybody wear a polka-dot dress to teach a class? That's going to bug me to death. I can't look at those polka dots all day. I'll get a migraine!" And the person next to you either fell in with your grousing, or nodded sympathetically and tried to ignore you.

The point I try to make is that attitude is infectious. We either lift each other up, or bring each other down. You probably know people who can dampen the spirit of an entire group with a grimace and a half-dozen well chosen words. They are like leaches, sucking on your attitude. They pull you down before you can defend yourself. They drain your happiness. As our mothers used to warn, be careful of the company you keep.

Attitude Is a Choice

No one has a perfect attitude. Even the most optimistic people experience break-through negativity and fear, often from thinking too much about their own troubles. And people certainly have a right to express their disappointments. However, after the third or fourth time, I want to say, "Get over it!" It's been proven that smiling diminishes depression and that laughter promotes good health. If you aren't eaten up with cancer, recovering from brain surgery, or confined to your death bed, *get over it.*

We go after negative news like thirsty dogs lapping up water. We read the newspaper and talk to each other about the sensational stories. Rarely do we exchange grilling recipes from the Sunday food section, or openly admire someone featured in a human-interest article. We migrate to the negative because it's more exciting. But remember this: persistent negative thinking is an abuse of the mind.

There are many uplifting stories. Cling to them. Leave behind the "My baby is cheating on me" songs. Divorce the negative past. Today is the first day of the rest of your life—a new beginning. Celebrate it as you would the New Year.

When my friend, Barry, was diagnosed with cancer, he made a conscious decision not to be sick. He and his wife, Linda, elected to view the entire situation as simply an inconvenience. Linda's style of managing the family was very positive. Everything in the household continued unchanged. Barry never stopped playing tennis, his favorite sport.

I watched and wondered. It was gratifying to see Barry's family rally behind him and have the grace to keep going in the face of the disease. This conscious choice on the part of the entire family made it possible for Barry to believe that he was going to be okay. Eventually, he recovered.

Sometimes choice eludes us. Children in particular can choose from only those reactions and behaviors that are modeled for them. When they survive extremely traumatic childhood experiences, I often wonder where the resilience came from.

When Sabrina was five years old, her grandfather started fondling her. As the years went by, the abuse became more and more frequent and intense. Sabrina is a people-pleaser today. That attribute as a child probably kept her from telling her family about the abuse.

I hope that Sabrina's story will hop off of the page and into your soul the way it penetrated mine. Today her voice is cheery, her smile is contagious and her love is vast. When I was overcome by anxiety during our interview, she soothed my tears. The pain I felt listening to her story was like a speck of sand compared to her lifetime of emotional agony.

Best-selling author and minister Joyce Meyer notes that many people are controlled by what she terms *approval addiction*. She explains, "Approval becomes something they believe they cannot live without. If they have it, they are happy and feel good about themselves and others, but if they don't, they are depressed and critical."

In seeking approval and happiness from her family, Sabrina kept her grandfather's fondling a secret for years. Today, looking back, she says she didn't know where to go.

When she was 19, Sabrina's grandfather passed away. Only then did she tell her family about the abuse. For years, she built walls and blocked people out, afraid they might find out about the abuse. In letting go of her approval addiction, Sabrina was able to tear down the barriers between a lifetime of lies and feeling good about herself.

After the birth of her second child, during the third of four marriages, Sabrina fell into a deep depression. She spent day and night on the living-room sofa, refusing to eat, bathe or respond.

Finally, she was hospitalized. Doctors blamed her condition on postpartum depression, which they later learned was stacked on top of a far more debilitating clinical depression.

After years of counseling and therapy, Sabrina is in the healing phase of her life. She is the proud mother of three children, with a heart full of love and devotion—a Christian woman harboring no grudges or hatred.

Attitude Produces Heroes

We are living in a world of heroes. The Jessica Lynch stories move us, and should. Jessica's ordeal as a prisoner of war in Iraq and her subsequent rescue and rehabilitation are very moving. But look around. Some of the ordinary folks in your work environment and circle of friends are heroes, too. One of mine is Maria.

Maria is a member of my social circle and a wonderful friend. When my family and I are guests in her home, her spirit and zest for life know no bounds. She and her husband, Paul, spend hours preparing an abundance of food for their frequent feasts. Both entertain with great poise, friendliness, enthusiasm, and spirit. The Italian in Maria comes out as she shoves bits of food in your mouth, saying, "Try this, you'll love it!" Yet underneath the fashionable clothes and jewelry of this strikingly beautiful woman lies a once-broken spirit.

Maria's father was an alcoholic and her mother, an immigrant from Italy who could not speak English, was manic-depressive. Her mother worked hard as a seamstress to support the family, but only brought home a few thousand dollars a year. The family depended on food stamps. Young Maria yearned for a normal life, which to her meant coming home from school and playing with the neighborhood kids until dusk.

At 17, Maria learned from her brother that her mother had tried to commit suicide. She had given up, but Maria and her siblings did not. As their mother became increasingly sick, they banded together, supported one another and moved forward.

Maria lost contact with her father, but she survived and gained strength from her childhood and adolescent experiences. Later in life, counseling helped her overcome the painful memories of her difficult upbringing, her mother's illness and her father's alcoholism. "I had to stop the cycle. I wasn't going to repeat the story," she says.

When Maria married Scott, a man with a seemingly perfect life, his parents became her parents. Maria and Scott's four children were soon living her childhood dream. They came home to a real neighborhood where they experienced a sense of security and belonging.

Then one day, Maria's perfect existence began to unravel. After a routine examination, Scott's physician asked to perform some additional tests. The results were devastating. Scott was diagnosed with an advanced cancer and given only a few months to survive.

"I remember sitting in the hospital waiting room, thinking how surreal the entire experience was. I couldn't believe it was happening," Maria recalled.

Scott died one year and three days after his diagnosis.

Maria's children were still young and had many questions as they struggled to deal with their father's death. Maria remembers one of her sons renouncing candy because he didn't want to be "sick like Daddy."

In retrospect, Maria offers the following advice to parents:

- Reassure the dying person that you will be able to carry on. Maria did household repairs in front of Scott. He became convinced that she could accomplish anything.

- Talk openly about the illness—no baby talk. Make your explanations age appropriate.

- When people come to you with horror stories, be strong.

- Crying is okay, but so is laughing.

- Don't feel guilty about being alive and seeing your kids grow up.

- When you feel sad, let your children know that you are venting. At the same time, let them know you are strong and will take care of them.

- Don't stop talking about the deceased parent (or other loved one). Silence multiplies the effects of the loss, whereas talking keeps that person's spirit alive.

Years later, Maria remarried, but she has always endeavored to keep Scot's spirit alive in the eyes of their children. Pictures of Scott are displayed throughout the home. Maria's new husband plays an integral role in maintaining Scott's memory with comments like, "Your dad was a smart man," and "Your father was a good runner."

Another hero of mine is Paula. When she was a young girl, Paula's legs started turning black. Doctors didn't have a diagnosis and couldn't find any reason for the deterioration of her legs. To stop the corrosion and prevent it from spreading to other parts of her body, doctors chose to amputate both legs.

Despite growing up around peers who could run circles around her, Paula chose not to feel sorry for herself. She never felt "different," nor was she picked on by other kids.

"I truly didn't know what I was missing," she says.

Her attitude about the situation is amazing. While many people would have become bitter, Paula has always kept her head high and has never allowed her condition to hold her back. In fact, for years she taught swimming lessons. She earned instructor certification and trained students from the deck of the pool.

Before you finish this book, you will read numerous stories that illustrate the importance of attitude. I teach and coach a great many people in my profession, and I have found their experiences highly instructive. It is important to understand how other people handle life's challenges—to identify and emulate role models. However, it is also important to look within and determine the state of your own attitude. Only through self-understanding can you begin to develop a positive attitude capable of prevailing in difficult circumstances. Self-assessment is the subject of the next chapter.

Exercise #1

The Flip-Side Technique

Have you thought to yourself, while getting ready for an important event, "I have nothing to wear"? Articulating the flip-side of that negative thought would have helped you to appreciate the resources you actually had. After all, having nothing to wear is not like hearing a physician deliver bad news, or getting *the* dreaded phone call in the middle of the night. In literal terms, having "nothing to wear" suggests poverty and, thankfully, real poverty is not the problem you faced.

I have visited orphanages and seen poverty up close. Some of my family's happiest days followed our return from Russia with our newly adopted daughter. We could not get the images of poverty out of our minds. While preparing to return home, we decided to leave behind our belongings—clothes, personal effects, even money. In the New York airport waiting for the next flight home, we had to count pennies to buy a hamburger at McDonalds. Credit cards were not accepted at fast food establishments in those days and we were ravenous. It was probably good for us to get a taste (no pun intended) of what poverty *really* feels like.

At any rate, the flip-side of "I have nothing to wear" might be, "I know I can be creative and put together an outfit for this event," or "I can manage this time, and next weekend I'll get my wardrobe in shape so that I won't face this situation again."

Try it. If you feel a little foolish—like a Pollyanna—don't let that stop you. There's nothing foolish about positive thinking. Once you develop the knack, your life will get so much better , you won't care whom you resemble. Having a positive attitude relieves stress, suffering, aggravation, and frowns!

Objective:

To experience and express the positive "flip-side" of any negative thought.

Materials:

none, other than your creativity.

Time required:

Approximately 10 minutes

Procedure:

1. Recall the first negative thought that came into your mind when you awoke today.

2. Examine the truth of the thought for a few moments.

3. Turn the thought around and look at its "flip-side." Maybe it has several possible flip-sides. Think about each of them.

4. Write down as many flip-side thoughts as you can in 5 minutes.

More Examples:

Thought: "Another dreary, rainy day." Flip side: "Rain will bring the flowers."

Thought: "I am miserable. "Flip side: "I don't have to be miserable. I am choosing to be miserable. I can make a different choice."

Thought: "I am angry." Flip side: "Why am I angry? How can I resolve this problem?"

Very often we live with negative circumstances, not because we have no choice, but because we haven't engaged our brains and emotions to see things differently. Dig deep. You can often see a brighter side of life by merely changing around a few thoughts or words.

STOP

Think about what you have learned from this chapter. Review your reactions and decide how you will use this information.

2

Examining Your Attitude

Like most kids, I used to sit in school and daydream. I would also try to block out or neutralize interruptions— even the teacher sometimes. I pictured a haven inside my mind, surrounded by a cubicle. No one could see in and I didn't have to look out unless I chose to. Inside this mental cubicle, I imagined small compartments—drawers, boxes, closets—that housed individual concerns, such as Mom, Dad, church, school, skiing, a specific conflict with my sister, a social event I was planning, or a test I was worried about. Every issue and concern had its own unique space.

I often began these mental escapes with a series of chants, much like the relaxation exercises we know today. To clear my mind so that I could begin to daydream, or work on a particular problem, I would picture any compartments that were worrying or distracting me and order them evacuated. I would say to myself: "Clear out that drawer. Clear out that spot. Clear out that closet." If my mind obeyed those commands, which it usually did, I would see the distracting issues swept away, at least temporarily.

To my knowledge, I had never seen an office cubicle, as my dad worked at the time in an Oregon lumberyard and my mom worked in a glove factory. If I behaved like this in today's world, I'd probably be taking medication for obsessive-compulsive behaviors—or some other "treatable" problem.

Your attitude is reflected in your behavior. If you believe that you have an attitude problem, or others have suggested that your attitude needs improvement, the first thing you need to do is make an honest appraisal of the situations that precipitate these complaints and the behaviors through which your attitude is being expressed.

Have you been blowing up at the office when work isn't completed on time or to your satisfaction? Do you become indignant in restaurants when the service is less than stellar? Do you drive everyone crazy sweating the small stuff, like how the dishwasher is loaded, or the length of your supervisor's lunch breaks? What behaviors provoke comments about your attitude? What do your coworkers, spouse, and children say?

If you are a procrastinator, you probably procrastinate at home as well as at work. If you are a lackadaisical person, chances are your indolence affects all areas of your life. If you are supersensitive to criticism and frequently become defensive, you will tend to provoke wariness wherever you go. If you really want to know how other people perceive your attitude, ask and observe. The information is readily available.

Indifference, Impatience and Egotism

How responsive are you to the needs of others? When family members, customers or colleagues come to you with concerns or questions, do you give them your undivided attention and take them seriously? Do you make an effort to reach inside yourself for a little empathy? Or is your manner distracted, offhanded or dismissive? Nothing is more frustrating than trying to engage a person who doesn't care. A common example is standing in line at a service counter where the lone employee is either on the phone, serving another customer, or otherwise occupied, and completely ignores your presence—no eye contact, no acknowledgment, no indication that you even exist. Sullen indifference seems to be the norm among teenagers juggling minimum-wage jobs, but far too many adults exhibit the same cold insensitivity.

Maybe you have an attitude of self-importance that gives people the impression you care only about your own experiences or opinions. Poor listening is often a symptom of self-involvement in the extreme. How often has someone inquired about your well-being in such a preoccupied manner that if you answered, "I'm okay, but my hemorrhoids are flaring up," they'd probably answer, "Great, give my best to Marge!" Whether in business or personal life, the highest compliment you can pay someone is to really listen—to give the person your undivided attention. Good listening is a hallmark of empathy.

An attitude of superiority turns some people into fulltime critics who take it upon themselves to evaluate anything and everything that passes within view. Other manifestations are aloofness, disdain and haughty disinterest.

Impatience is an attitude that I see a lot these days. We hurry through life—picking up the kids, doing the laundry, paying the bills, rushing off to earn another day's wages. Sometimes we speed around so fast that we don't bother to consider how (or whether) our activities matter. Impatient people easily become angry, demanding, complaining people.

In the book, *The Power of Patience,* author M.J. Ryan describes an organized and efficient woman who was getting ready to run a number of errands with her husband. In an effort to speed the process, she divided the list—half for her husband, half for her. But her husband protested, saying, "I thought the point was to do these things together." That incident taught the woman that "the journey is as important as the destination." In grade school, students get stickers for being the first to finish an assignment. But in the real world of adulthood, rushing through life can spoil the pleasure. Take the time to step back, relax and enjoy the process.

Laziness, Disrespect and Other Office Attitudes

A common attitude problem in many companies is disrespect. Maybe you have a reputation for bad-mouthing the company that employs you. It's foolish to work for a company that you do not support. If you can't speak well of your company, you would be better off quitting to look for other employment. Employees should be informed about their company and its products—they should be walking advertisements. I cannot tell you how many people I interview who know next to nothing about the company that employs them. They have neither the interest nor the initiative to inform themselves. Attitudes like this are like big flashing neon signs of complacence. No one misses them.

I teach a course called "We Are All Receptionists," in which I tell people that we should be as gracious at our place of business as we are to guests in our homes. When we have visitors at home, we offer them something to drink and a comfortable place to sit. We look our guests in the eye and listen to what they have to say. We don't often show the same respect at the office. We believe that it's the receptionist's job to receive clients. Professional receptionists are good with people and have chosen this occupation, so let them handle it.

Office visitors should always be escorted to their destination, not left to wander the halls. Physically walk them to the office of the person they are there to see. Professionals such as physicians, lawyers, accountants, financial advisors and human resource managers should all accept that they, too, are receptionists. Whether in the treatment room or conference room, you owe it to the other person to listen and to focus on their needs and concerns. The last call of the day should be answered with the same zeal as the first. The patient just before lunch should be handled as well as the first patient of the day. If these attitudes don't come naturally, this is an area on which to focus.

I hear a lot of professional people discussing customers, clients and patients in highly unprofessional ways. What happened to the old fashioned notion of confidentiality? If customers and patients could hear the chatter that goes on just beyond earshot, they would probably take their business elsewhere. Participating in gossip is a related problem, and horribly contagious.

Super-casual attire and behavior in the workplace, when tolerated or encouraged, sometimes breed sloppy, sluggish attitudes. I work with large corporations that have dress-down days. Studies have shown that when people do not dress appropriately for their careers, they are not as productive as when they dress professionally. Dressing professionally can rev up a sluggish attitude. It can also improve the way you are treated. I read of a study in which a group of teachers was divided into two subgroups. One subgroup dressed professionally every day. The other subgroup wore casual attire, including jeans. At the end of the 10-week trial, the casually dressed teachers reported receiving negative treatment, including threats from students. The professionally dressed teachers reported positive, respectful treatment.

A Quick Attitude Assessment

If you are not sure about the source of your attitude problems, evaluate your behavior by answering the following questions. Write down your answers and explore each area thoroughly.

1. *How do you typically interact with others?*

   Are you a good listener or do you monopolize conversations? Do you show an interest in other people and their activities, or is the focus always on you? Are you congenial, sarcastic, humble, arrogant, thoughtful, meek, fun to be with, or a complainer?

2. *How well do you perform in your job?*

   Ask five coworkers to assess your performance. You can do this informally, but make sure you choose people who will be straight with you. Tell them you need the information to help you plan a self-improvement program. Listen carefully for comments related to attitude.

3. *What are your three biggest worries?*

   Some worries are temporary and situational, such as worrying that you'll be late for a meeting because of traffic. Other worries are recurring and deep-seated, such as persistent apprehension over finances or job performance. Pick chronic worries, things that bother you on a more-or-less constant basis. How do these worries affect your attitude? How do they color the way you approach activities and interact with other people? Trace each concern back in time as far as you can until you understand where it originates. Finally, begin to think of ways to address each worry so that it won't be such a burden and a drag on your attitude. The best way to reduce anxiety is through action.

4. In what manner do you give and receive compliments?

Some people are stingy with compliments. They are reluctant to praise the people around them, even when praise is richly deserved. Other people think that the value of praise is overrated, particularly in the workplace. After all, performing well is our job—it's what we were hired to do. You probably know a few people who are generous with compliments. They seem to enjoy making others feel good by noticing their successes and appearance and expressing genuine appreciation for even the smallest favor. What about you? Which description best fits you?

Many of us find it very difficult to graciously receive compliments. We are so used to thinking and saying negative things to ourselves, we feel compelled to discount praise when we hear it from others. When a friend says, "These are great brownies. I've never had better," we respond with comments like, "Well, they are kind of dry. You should've had the moist ones I made last week ." The inability to accept compliments and feel good about them is often symptomatic of an attitude of unworthiness. Believing yourself unworthy can in turn lead to all kinds of annoying, self-deprecating behaviors.

5. How do you react in conflict situations?

Conflict is an inevitable fact of daily life. People have different opinions, different values and different ways of doing things. If two kids both want the last cookie, they bicker. If two employees both want the same vacation week, and only one can be gone from the office, they argue. How do you react to conflict? Do you go into attack mode at the first sign of trouble? Do you quickly retreat in fear? Or do you enter most conflicts with an open mind, ready to put forth the effort to work things out? Rest assured, your typical style of managing conflict colors every facet of your attitude.

6. How does your behavior at work differ from your behavior at home?

Chances are if you are a negative thinker at home, then the same holds true at work. However, that's not always the case. If you are dealing with extremely difficult circumstances at home, your job may become a haven where you can express your talents and actualize your potential. Conversely, if your job is boring, unpleasant, or highly stressful, you may become a "different person" at home. Since this is a self-assessment, the key is to identify specific attitudinal differences so you will know where to focus your efforts.

If you answer these questions honestly, you will begin to see a pattern. That pattern will contain clues to the source of your attitude problems and, if not the source, then the triggers—the circumstances that send you plunging into anger, bitterness or despair.

Once you have identified the trigger behaviors, try to understand the roots of your responses. For example, if you use sarcasm to put people down when they disagree with you, trace that behavior back as far as you can. Attitude habits begin forming in childhood. Perhaps one of your parents modeled sarcastic behavior and you accepted and absorbed it. Once I saw a child wearing a T-shirt that read, "underachiever and proud of it" from *The Simpsons* TV show. It broke my heart, and I wondered how he could ever hope to become a successful student wearing that shirt. And if he didn't become a successful student, how could he become a successful businessperson, scientist, firefighter, or technology worker? Oh, I know, he might have been a great student who was indulging in a little harmless self-deprecation. But maybe not. Maybe he actually thought underachievement was cool. Attitudes begin early!

Accepting Responsibility

People often argue that their attitudes were created by other people. That's pure nonsense. Your attitude is *your* responsibility. It doesn't belong to anyone else. Don't attribute your behavior to what someone else did to you. The fact that your boss spoke harshly to you in the morning is no excuse for running roughshod over every person you encounter throughout the day.

At 17, I blamed my involvement with drugs on the fact that my father was gone and my mother was dead. No matter how you look at them, those excuses don't fly. A lot of teenagers lead difficult lives but don't turn to alcohol and drugs. And many folks who enjoy numerous social and economic advantages become users and addicts. At any rate, the abuse to my body eventually caused me to hit rock bottom, stop self-medicating and begin a new life.

Chances are, if you are blaming others for your attitude, you need to do a "checkup from the neck up." I once knew a prosperous professional man in his late forties who was single, reasonably attractive, well educated and financially secure, and needed his head examined in the worst way. He lived in a custom home in a very desirable neighborhood, yet whined incessantly that his long-dead parents had left his older sister exactly half of their ample estate even though she lived in a rent-controlled apartment and "didn't need the money." Granted, this is an extreme example, but you get the idea. If this guy was miserable (and he often seemed to be), it was because of what he did to himself, not what his parents did to him. One of the most important indications of maturity, in my opinion, is reaching the point where you can accept and appreciate your parents just as they are, or were, and stop blaming them for your problems. As long as you are unable to do that without reservation, you simply don't have both feet in adulthood.

As unpleasant circumstances enter your life, be aware that you have choices. Don't just fall aimlessly into some automatic way of operating. You might as well give in to disaster. Whatever happened, it is not *his* fault, *her* fault or *their* fault. The choice of reactions begins and ends with you. You have the power to respond in any way you choose.

It's all in your head. *Your* head, not someone else's. If you are a negative person, it's because you have negative, self-defeating thoughts. If you wallow in bitterness and resentment, negative, self-defeating thoughts are running your life. Your attitude defines you. If you don't believe that it does, ask the people around you.

Exercise #2

Data Dump

This activity resembles a computer data dump—hence its name. It is also similar to a thorough housecleaning. I often liken it to clearing out and organizing a closet.

The client and I sit down at a conference table with a huge stack of index cards. I instruct the client to write down fleeting thoughts, one per card, in response to topics that I announce. The client writes the first thought that comes to mind, and then as many more thoughts as possible before I announce the next topic. Each thought goes on a separate card. Topics are more or less complicated depending upon what is happening in the client's life, so it may take two cards or 10.

We continue this process in several additional 30-minute sessions. The topics are potentially repetitive to give the client every opportunity to get important information out.

Next, we arrange the cards in stacks according to the concern or theme expressed. For example, if thoughts related to being overweight are mentioned in relation to 12 different topics, all 12 cards go in the same stack. After we get the stacks in order, we can readily see a pattern of concerns and issues. These are then prioritized and goals and action plans developed to deal with the most important.

The following exercise has been modified to allow you to complete a data dump on your own, without a facilitator. However, you always have the option of asking a friend or professional counselor to work with you.

Objectives

In this exercise you will:
- Clean out the furthest corners of your mind.
- Examine all the thoughts and issues
  you are presently dealing with.
- Eliminate relatively unimportant matters.
- Put back *only* that which is important,
  and in an orderly fashion.
- Develop a plan for dealing with important issues.
- Focus your attention on priority issues.

Materials

Approximately 300 3x5 index cards

Time required

30-minute sessions on most days for approximately two to four weeks

Procedure

1. Go through the topic list and eliminate topics that are totally irrelevant. For example, if you have never been married, eliminate "In-laws."

2. Select a topic.

3. Write the first thought that comes to your mind concerning that topic. Push the card aside. Take a second card and write your second thought. Continue in this manner for as long as you continue to have discrete thoughts on the topic.

4. Select the next topic and repeat the process. Address no more than 10 topics a day from the remaining list. Write feverishly about each topic, recording each thought on a separate card. *Do not go back into the stacks and change answers, or even think about them, until the sorting exercise* (step 5).

5. Sort the cards into stacks by concern or issue. Be careful not to group multiple concerns in a single stack. For instance, if you described four discrete issues involving your spouse—long work hours, lack of intimacy, different parenting styles and excessive drinking—they belong in four separate stacks. Only when two or more are related (if, say, the lack of intimacy stems from your spouse's long work hours), do they go in the same stack.

6. Further sort the stacks into five groups labeled 1, 2, 3, 4 and 5, with the 1's being the most important and the 5's being the least important.

7. Place the 4's and 5's in sealed envelopes and put them away for one year.

8. Place the 3's in a sealed envelope for 6 months.

9. Examine and prioritize the 1's and 2's. Begin setting goals and developing action plans to deal with them. Cross them off the list as they are resolved.

10. At the end of 6 months, begin addressing those 3's that have not resolved themselves in the meantime. Sometimes they seem marginal after getting through the important issues, so toss them if you wish.

11. After one year, decide which 4's and 5's warrant further attention. (Many people choose to "divorce" their 4's and 5's without even opening those envelopes.)

Topic List

Disappointments
Spiritual matters
Boats
Cars
Habits
Careers
Hobbies

Accomplishments
In-laws
Dating
Mini-trips
Parents
Tennis
Golf
Running
Sports
Siblings
Spare time
Direction of your life
Studying
Health
Wellness
Focus
Drugs
Alcohol
Relationships
House
Retirement
Organizations
Vacations
Your life's work
Your passion in life
Marriage
Children
Religion
Exercise
Patterns in your life
Ten things that make you happy
Rental property
Relaxation
Quiet time
Future
Professionalism
Clothing/wardrobe

Swimming
Rowing
Diving
Money
School
Identity
Who do I want to be?
Who did my parents want me to be?
Ten things I like about my partner
Love
Laughter
How would my spouse describe me?
Bills
Commitments
Emotional stability
Stresses
Time
I love life because…
Dreams
Divorce
Fussing
Quarrelling
Attitudes
What my children will say about me after I die
Change
Compassion
I hate life because…
I need to stop whining and start doing…
Something that changed me forever
My mentors are…
Changes I want to make

STOP

Think about what you have learned from this chapter. Review your reactions and decide how you will use this information.

3

Deciding to Change

Several physicians remarked that my running three to seven miles at a stretch during periods of illness was impossible. Most of the lupus patients I have talked to claim that running the vacuum cleaner can put them in bed for two days. I experienced comparable states of exhaustion and from time to time reluctantly gave in to them, but for the most part was determined to keep going. My desire to conquer my illness led to periods of remission. It was during the pity parties that I hurt the worst and was hospitalized the most.

Decide how you want your attitude to function from this day forward. You will be a happier person knowing that you have *chosen* how you intend to think and react, rather than accepted whatever your subconscious mind or spontaneity produced. You will feel better about yourself if you are proactive and take responsibility for your disposition and happiness.

By choosing to develop a positive attitude, you are agreeing to respond to negative situations by deliberately looking for the hidden advantages and molding beneficial outcomes. You are choosing to make lemonade out of lemons. You will be more loving and you will feel better. You will not be depressed all the time, and you will begin to see that there are a lot of people in whose lives you can make a difference, and they can make a difference in yours.

I realize that changes like these are difficult. It is very challenging to remain positive in a cold, negative world. Newspapers and the media sensationalize bad news. It's part of the "news as entertainment" mentality that currently pervades TV and many print news sources as well. If it isn't horrible, we don't read it. If it isn't titillating, we don't respond to it. If it isn't shocking, we don't repeat it. The answer, of course, is to limit your exposure to negative news until such time as you feel strong enough to withstand its influence. For example, I know several people who no longer watch network news broadcasts. They deplore the direction that the networks have taken—becoming increasingly tabloid over the years. They prefer straight news to sensationalized drama mixed with mindless commercials.

This is about choice. You must determine how you want to be. You must decide that you will not feel gloomy every time it rains. You will not get worried every time your boss frowns at you. You will not teeter on the edge of depression every time someone disappoints you. Your new intention will be to look for the positive in every situation.

I have two friends, Jeff and Jim, who always can be counted on to express a positive outlook on life. Despite any problems going on at home or work, every time I ask Jeff how he is doing, he replies, "Never better." I can depend on that answer whenever I come in contact with him. Even when the chips are down, he is, "Never better."

As for Jim, this most giving man always has a smile on his face and a positive comment for others, even in the midst of the worst personal struggles. Each time I inquire, he always responds, "It's all good," and for him it is. He has the ability to find the silver lining behind any circumstance that comes his way. He is a true inspiration. I think of them both when I am trying to overcome my own *stinkin' thinkin'*.

Taking Charge

What do you want from life? What sort of person do you want to be? What interests and desires drive you? Do you want professional success, a busy social life, spiritual growth, travel? And what about your character? How do you want people to describe you to their friends?

Don't make excuses that the actions or words of others stand in your way. If you have a tendency to focus on all of the reasons why you *can't* accomplish your goals, force yourself to stop these pessimistic thoughts. Write down your negative, self-defeating thoughts. Then rewrite them, changing them into positive thoughts. For example, if a little voice in your head tells you, "I blew the interview so I'll never get the promotion," train it to say instead, "I did the best I could in the interview and I'll do even better next time."

Think of obstacles as opportunities, challenges and learning experiences. Don't limit yourself. *Believe in yourself.* Decide what you want to do and go after it. No excuses! You are what you think you are!

Who Do You Want to Be?

In order to gain full control of your hopes and dreams, you must begin to ask questions about who you are and who you want to be. What kind of spouse are you, and what kind of parent? What visions do you want to actualize in your professional, social and family life? In relationships, couples like to say that they give 50-50, when in reality they give 110 percent some days and 40 percent others. They also tell me, "I don't want to do (a certain thing) because that will be perceived as giving in, and I don't want my partner to think that I will respond to his (or her) every demand." It's not about him or her. It's about *you*. It is so important to look into your heart, mind and soul and determine who you want to be.

In our goal-driven society, we're accustomed to setting our sights on material aspirations—the house, the car, the investment portfolio. Some of us wisely develop professional ambitions to match our material desires, others of us never do and either go into debt acquiring the things we want or merely dream about them. This book is not about your job or your house, except to the degree that attitude affects them. It is about the kind of person you intend to be in the good times and bad. So when I ask you to define the person you want to be, I'm asking you to dig deeper than the résumé and the pocketbook. I want you to examine your thoughts and feelings, your fortitude and resilience, your empathy and assertiveness. These are the qualities that drive your professional and material goals and that determine how you will respond when a crisis hits, as the following example illustrates.

Growing up, Susan was lucky enough to have encouraging parents who instilled in her a sense of humor, respect for hard work, and abiding faith. Susan and her sisters knew that there was nothing they could not accomplish if they put their minds to it.

Throughout her life, Susan's spirit has been put to the test. She experienced four failed pregnancies, then finally adopted two beautiful little girls from China. Later her husband died of leukemia.

When her husband became ill, the two girls went to live with Susan's sister while Susan cared for their father. After a long period during which he was unresponsive, Susan told her husband it was okay for him to die. Susan told me that the strong support of family, church and friends gave her the strength to move on. I believe the strength of Susan's character played an equally important role.

The Power of Desire

When I go on about the person you *want* to be and the kind of attitude you must *want* to have, I'm assuming that you would not be reading this book if you did not see value in the whole notion of Attitude Therapy. But let me caution you: changes in attitude don't come easily. They require hard work (more about that in a later chapter) and intense desire. You have to yearn for the solid feeling of attitudinal strength the way you yearn for wealth. You have to crave it like you crave sex or chocolate. Desire is mandatory. A lukewarm, halfhearted commitment to change won't produce much of anything. You must have passion.

In *The Magic of Believing*, Claude M. Bristol observes that relatively few people know what they actually want in life. Most people seem to accept their positions as fated and are content to fill whatever roles come their way. They don't make an effort to abandon those niches and improve themselves and their circumstances. In his words, "Many engage in wishful thinking, but wishful thinking in itself is without effect simply because the power factor is missing."

Bristol asserts that, until you come across a completely motivated and focused individual, you don't know the power of desire. Focused people attract the very things they desire by fixing their thoughts and imaginations upon them. They use their subconscious minds to magnetize and transmit to their conscious minds electrifying visions of the objects they desire.

Desire—the "power factor"—is a product of your emotional brain, along with love, excitement, longing, devotion and other feelings. It's been said that emotions are the "door to learning," because when a student gets excited about a subject, the subject opens up and the student becomes absorbed in it. Learning is drudgery for the complacent, but a playground for the passionate. The same is true of change. Changing anything about yourself or your life can be very difficult if desire is missing or compromised. But if desire is strong, motivation and focus will propel you toward your goals.

As you examine your attitudes and values and begin to develop a plan for change, try to maintain a spirit of openness—like the journalist who flew to Japan to interview a monk regarding Zen-Buddhism. Just before the interview, the monk offered the journalist hot tea. He handed the man a teacup and started pouring. As the liquid reached the rim of the glass, he continued to pour. The tea overflowed onto the floor. The journalist said, "Stop pouring. My cup is overflowing." The monk replied, "Your cup is very much like you. It is too full to receive any more tea."

If you approach Attitude Therapy too full to receive what you need or wish to receive, how will you learn? Start with an open, yielding attitude and build from there.

Role Models and Mentors

An excellent way to create a blueprint for the kind of attitude you hope to develop is to examine the attitudes and outlooks of people you hold in high esteem. Think about this for a few moments. Then, make a list of the individuals you most admire. Choose one name from the list, and write down the strengths and exemplary qualities of that person. Maybe you respect the person's honesty, integrity, creative ability, or sense of humor. Compare these qualities to your own profile and identify areas where you need to focus in order to be more like this person. Pick a second name from the list and go through the same exercise.

Finally, pick the most influential person from the list and, if he or she is still living, call and express your appreciation—or write a letter of gratitude. Stay in touch and continue to be influenced. Be as thirsty for positive influence as you would be for water in a hot, dry desert.

To my good fortune, I have had many mentors in my life who have nourished me with their bright-side-of-life philosophy. One of those was my former pastor. I began attending church when I was a very young girl and for many years had the same wonderful minister. I was blessed by his influence and learned many positive ideals and concepts from him that I am taking with me through life.

If you can find someone out there with exemplary qualities—a positive individual whose character you would like to mirror—simply ask that person to be your mentor. Study your mentor and learn from him or her. Have discussions, ask for advice, and listen to your mentor's stories. Most of us hunger to hear uplifting stories from positive role models, much as our children love to hear what we have experienced. How else do we learn but by example?

If you have never faced the demise of a business or stared your own death in the face, I offer this advice: learn from those who have. I have experienced both and survived. It does not matter if you are 30 or 65, you have the ability to learn from others.

Recently I talked with my friend, Cissy, who was diagnosed with Multiple Sclerosis. A dominant theme in our conversation was the support she received from her family. They sustained her through her illness. She says that if she had not been diagnosed with MS, she might never have known the intensity of her family's love and support. Being stricken with a serious illness in early adulthood helped her appreciate the value of life.

Cissy described her fear that every day would be the same, but was able to look on the positive side and say to herself, "I am here today. I am performing on this level today. I am going to shut out the fears and enjoy the quality of life I have."

With a positive attitude, illness can make the quality of life even sweeter. It reminds us that life is too great a privilege to be taken for granted. Like I always say, if you want to find out who you are, get sick.

It's Up to You

One day I was out for a walk with my daughters, Molly and Maggie, when Maggie paused at the foot of a bridge in our path. She hesitated to cross the bridge, expressing a fear that she might die. Five-year-old Molly looked at Maggie and said, "The river is there, but whether you look at it, or pretend it's not there, is up to you."

Life is a mix of joy and sorrow, success and failure, ecstasy and heartbreak. While you focus on the highs, prepare for the lows, because they will come whether you are ready for them or not. Get your attitude in tip-top shape so that the buoyancy of your outlook will carry you over those inevitable valleys.

Remember, no matter what your life is like now, you have the power to make positive change and create the life you really want. Attitude is everything.

Exercise #3

Daily Activity Inventory

Objectives

This exercise is designed to help you develop greater choice in your daily activities, both in terms of what you do, and your attitude toward what you do.

Materials

Writing materials or computer

Time required

About 30 minutes

Procedure

1. Think about all the things you do on a typical weekday. (As an alternative, focus on a typical weekend, but don't try to do both at once.) Make a list of the separate tasks and activities you usually perform during the day. It may help to visualize yourself going through the day and list items in chronological order.

2. Go back over the completed list and decide which items represent things you *must* do and which represent things you are in the *habit* of doing, but don't have to do. Put an "M" or an "H" beside each item.

3. Next, go through the list and answer the following questions in relation to each *must do* (M) item.

   • What is my usual attitude when doing (or contemplating) this activity?

   • What improvements in attitude would make this activity less stressful and more enjoyable?

4. Go through the list again and answer the following questions in relation to the *habit* (H) items.

• How do I or my family benefit from this activity?

• How could I use this time more productively?

5. Take action based on your answers. Coach yourself to think more positively about mandatory activities. Set goals to eliminate any habitual activities that you would like to replace. Immediately substitute a new activity for each one.

STOP

Think about what you have learned from this chapter. Review your reactions and decide how you will use this information.

4

Stop Complaining

During a routine hysterectomy, the surgeon removed a malignant tumor from the ovary of my good friend, Tami. When the doctor called Tami at 11 p.m. one evening to tell her the findings, she phoned me and I went straight over in my pajamas. Tami reacted at first with disbelief. This couldn't be happening again. She had first been diagnosed with cancer three years earlier, and this was the second recurrence in two years.

After gathering her thoughts, Tami set out on a mission to find out the best way to approach the situation. She told her three children that the family had hit another little bump in the road and explained that she would have to take medicine to recover. She refused to take it as a death sentence.

When she goes to the cancer unit for treatments, Tami looks at the other patients and wonders why she is there. She truly believes in her spirit that she belongs out walking in the sunshine where she can see the sky and hear the birds. Tami believes that she will recover, but in the event that she does not, she has learned a

***beautiful lesson from the experience and is teaching it to
her children: simple pleasures are the best.***

One of my goals in Attitude Therapy is to help people stop
complaining. Many of us go through our days complaining about
trivial matters such as the weather, traffic and the common cold.
We are a whining, sniveling society.

In this rich country, with so many blessings, I have heard
people come out of an ice cream shop complaining because their
favorite flavor was unavailable. I've seen a person leave a tennis
lesson complaining because the instructor went three minutes
over, and I've heard a Mercedes owner complain because the
car wash left spots on the windshield. These examples seem
humorous, sad and embarrassing all at the same time. How silly
they make us look.

While in a restaurant recently, I overheard several ladies
fussing about their Botox® injections. At another table, two grown
men were lamenting that they had to help their wives with the kids
on Saturday and couldn't play golf. They almost wept. I wanted
to go over and deliver the lecture I give my kids: "I will *not* put
up with you acting like a spoiled rotten South Hills* punk. Your
whining defines the person you are becoming. Do you like that
person?"

Weather Woes and Waiting

There are plenty of negative people out there, and never
enough positive ones. Think about the last time it rained. Someone
with whom you came in contact that day probably said, "Oh, it's
a miserable day." Another remarked, "I was fine until it started
raining," and someone else said, "I could do without all this rain."
It seems as though we complain to hear ourselves complain. If
someone startles you by saying, "It's a great day, how are you?"
you catch yourself thinking, "What is he taking? Is he on crack?
It's pouring down rain. This guy is soaking wet and thinks it's a
great day!"

---

* South Hills is the area in which we live

My little boy, Tate, is seven. He is the most positive, happy person in the world. One morning he ran to the window to see the rain. I thought he'd be bummed knowing soccer was cancelled. Instead, he said, "Mommy it's raining, but won't the flowers be pretty?" Tate employs the "flip-side technique" regarding almost every situation (See Chapter 1). He always gets up from the table and says with much enthusiasm, "Mom, this was the best food. Thank you."

If you want to assess the attitudes of people, make them wait in a line. Lines bring out the worst and the best in people. Waiting in line at a bank, or to pick up food for lunch, one person will respond positively while another will behave rudely, expressing anger and an it's-all-about-me attitude. The positive person has assessed the situation, recognized that nothing can be done about it and decided to chill out. The other person has become extremely anxious and lost control.

The Company You Keep

My husband and I used to travel and socialize with two of the sweetest, funniest people you would ever want to meet. However, the wife always tore down the husband. She would do it in groups and at the dinner table. She would do it privately in the ladies room with me. Whenever an opportunity arose, she would cut him down and say bad things about him. In some ways it was humorous—a little like "Saturday Night Live." But most of the time it was uncomfortable.

Sometimes I would find myself thinking, "Gosh, he does that?" (I'll call him Tom.) "Tom does that? My husband does that, too! You're complaining because Tom says that? Mine says that all the time." Afterwards, at home, I'd lie in the bed just as cold as a piece of ice, with my arms down at my sides. My neck would get stiff from staying on my side of the bed. My husband would say, "What's wrong?" and I would answer, "Nothing." To which he would respond, "No, no, no, what's wrong?" and again I would say, "Nothing."

We have to be selective about the people with whom we associate. A lot of our *stinkin' thinkin'* comes from the people we're around. As youngsters, we were all told by our parents that we are the company we keep. It's true, we do absorb verbal habits, behaviors and attitudes from the people with whom we associate.

We need to surround ourselves with friends we cherish who care equally about us. Ask yourself who are your real friends. Do you surround yourself with positive people who treat others with respect? People who talk negatively behind the backs of their friends and family members will do the same to you, right after you leave the room. Every minute you subject yourself to this type of negativity is another minute to be influenced by (if not programmed with) similar attitudes and behaviors. Growing up, I was surprised at how easily I picked up the mannerisms and slang of the kids with whom I hung out.

I adhere to the "white van philosophy," which goes something like this: if you drive a white van, you see all the other white vans on the road. If you have a bad attitude, you attract others with bad attitudes. If you have a good attitude, you attract positive people with good attitudes. To determine the relative state of your own attitude, take an objective look at the adults who choose to be around you.

Restaurant Ruminations

One morning at breakfast, the lady at the next table said to the waitress, "This is not my bill," and demanded the right one. With a smile, the waitress delivered the correct bill and an apology. The apology was not accepted. My husband remarked to the lady in jest, "Be glad you didn't get *our* bill (there were eight of us)." She ignored him. I get tickled at people who take life so seriously.

When the luck of the draw gives you a horrible server in a restaurant, instead of whispering and moaning to your companions, take direct action to change the situation. Just because you are training yourself to have a good attitude doesn't mean you have to sit around and act like you want to be abused. Put a stop to unacceptable behaviors. Do it in a assertive, straightforward manner without exhibiting *stinkin' thinkin'* or a bad attitude. Say, "Pardon me. Have I done something to offend you, or are you just having a bad day?" Chances are the server will apologize and confess to being tired or overworked. If so, you can help the situation by just listening.

Recently I overheard two waitresses chatting in the ladies room of a restaurant. One said to the other, "Honey, they wouldn't let you off?" The waitress responded (obviously with a horrible cold), "There was no sense in asking. Last month they only gave me one day off when my mom died." I shuddered to think of being in her shoes. Eye-openers like this make me more tolerant of the attitudes of service workers.

Recently I was at a wonderful resort called the Greenbrier. I was in the library, writing. When I started feeling sleepy, I walked over to the library's small snack bar and asked the woman there if I could get a soft drink. She very sweetly said, "Sure," and apologized that the pop can was warm. As she gave me some ice, she explained that the bar wasn't open yet. I said, "I'm so sorry. How nice of you to help me out." The majority of employees would have pointed to the posted hours and told me to come back later. This woman's attitude and behavior were exceptional.

How to Be Taken Seriously

I make it a rule never to gripe and complain about things I cannot fix. The only time you will hear me complain is when I *can* do something about it, and then I will talk to the people involved. But I would rather quietly go about my business than go around grumbling and growling. One of the biggest benefits of this approach is that my husband takes me seriously any time I do complain.

At this point, you may be thinking, "Well, isn't she perfect!" Quite the contrary. Even though I teach Attitude Therapy and focus on attitude and believe that I have a good attitude, when I'm with cantankerous people who carry on about how this isn't working, or that isn't working, I'm tempted to jump right in there with them. But I have trained myself to be acutely aware of negative behavior and work daily to rise above the temptation to complain. As a consequence, my family stops everything and listens when they hear me fuss. I get more attention than you could ever imagine. I didn't establish the "no complaining" standard with that in mind, but being taken seriously when it counts is a wonderful fringe benefit. If I complained every day about something, people would quit listening to me. Because I try not to complain, I am taken very seriously when I do. The exception is my 15-year old son, Ryan, and the neatness of his bedroom, about which I fuss all the time.

You can make your day as rotten as you want by complaining from the time your feet hit the floor to the time you go to bed, or you can look for the good in everything in life and enjoy your days. I guarantee you will be happier if you choose the latter course. And I strongly suspect that you will live a longer and healthier life, too.

Dolly Parton always inspires me when she walks on to a stage. Once, when an interviewer asked how she maintained such a positive attitude, she explained that so many negative things had occurred in her life, she learned to look for the positive. That habit stayed with her over the years. She said, "I will continue signing autographs, I will continue being nice to people because the majority of people are nice and appreciate it. And the majority of people is what really got me here. Why would I gripe about it?"

Save It for the "Big One"

We all deal with hassles from time to time. But it is such a shame when people spend their days ranting incessantly about their troubles. Those who do are not in touch with the real meaning of life. I doubt that they have been through a life-threatening disease, divorce or other devastating circumstance.

I coach people who have terminal illnesses and are in continuous excruciating pain. I sometimes work with them for months and years without ever hearing them complain. I certainly do not hear them sniveling about the minor, superficial things the people in my own circle complain about. Apparently folks in dire situations have come to realize that whining doesn't accomplish anything. They have figured out that complaining ought to be saved for when "the big one" hits.

It is very important that you quit complaining about little issues in life. Develop a habit of talking about the good things. You will be a stronger, healthier individual, and when bigger events do come into your life, you will be able to handle them.

You will have the energy to manage them. You may have heard the statement, "The more you stir it, the worse it stinks." Well, the more you complain and whine about your problems, the worse they become. Attitude is not about what happens to you, it is about how you respond to what happens to you.

Finding the Cause

If you know (or suspect) that others view you as a chronic complainer, and you want to change, start with an honest appraisal of what causes you to zero in on the negatives in situations instead of the positives—the deficiencies instead of the attributes.

Perfectionism is one possible culprit. Excellence is a worthy goal, but it can lead to chronic dissatisfaction, which in turn often produces a great deal of nitpicking and complaining. Few people and things in life are perfect. If you are a perfectionist, concentrate on setting your performance standards a notch or two lower. The first person to benefit from more relaxed expectations will be you.

Lack of assertiveness is another common cause of chronic complaining. I'm not talking now about in-your-face complainers. Foot-stomping, fist-pounding complainers are beyond assertive, they are downright aggressive in making their dissatisfaction known. I'm talking about the sniveling complainers who talk in low tones and behind people's backs, but don't do anything to change the situation. Sometimes they have legitimate complaints, other times they seem to be on auto-pilot, but in either case they appear incapable of taking action. If that description fits you, I'd recommend assertiveness training to build your sense of self-worth and personal agency.

Finally, some complainers are simply very unhappy people who are determined to share their misery with the rest of the world on a more or less continual basis. This is a tough one to mitigate, but I think unhappy people often benefit from thinking less about themselves and more about others. One of the best ways to do that is through a few hours a week of volunteer work. Giving of yourself and your time can be very rewarding. The social contact helps, too. Beyond that, counseling may be in order.

When Complaining Is a Habit

Some of us become complainers because we hang around other complainers. Behaviors, even bad ones, can be surprisingly contagious. We seem to have a wired-in tendency to mirror one another. The good news is, that tendency produces empathy. The bad news is, we sometimes mimic undesirable behaviors until they become habits.

If your complaining is merely a bad habit, the best remedy is to replace it with a good habit. Habits take approximately 21 days to form, so that means whatever behavior you substitute for complaining has to be practiced religiously for three solid weeks. The obvious choice would be to substitute a positive comment for each complaint that you start to utter, but you could also substitute a smile, a few deep breaths, or a question. Keep in mind, however, that if you continue to associate regularly with other complainers, the change process could take considerably longer.

Exercise #4

Complaint Count

Objectives:

This exercise will help you:

- Become aware of how often in the course of a day you make complaining statements.

- Reduce complaining by taking charge of your thoughts.

Materials:

Pencil and a small notebook that will fit in your pocket or purse

Time required:

Continuous vigilance throughout the day for at least two weeks

Procedure:

1. Carry the pad with you wherever you go. Nobody needs to know what it is for.

2. Bright and early each morning, write the date at the top of a new page.

3. Pay attention to your interactions throughout the day. Every time you complain, make a tally mark on the page. Do this at the office, in the supermarket, in the car, at dinner—wherever you are. You will be absolutely mortified at the results.

4. Read a book or article on positive thinking, underlining specific ideas that will help you improve your attitude and lessen your complaining.

5. Begin another week of posting your tally marks. Compare the results from one week to the next and notice the improvement. You are becoming aware when the negative creeps into your mind and you are learning to conquer it.

6. Continue this exercise as long as you wish. *Things get better when you get better.*

STOP

Think about what you have learned from this chapter. Review your reactions and decide how you will use this information.

5

Making a Plan

Starting over isn't easy when it's the 30th time you've started over.

After my last bout with illness, drugs and lethargy, I started walking. I was weak, so at first one block was enough for me. But because I'm an overachiever, my self-talk was beating me up. I thought, If you can walk a block, you can walk a mile and, for that matter, why not run?

When I coach people, I remind them that success is about stepping out with the first stride. You have to have the will to do it, not necessarily the strength. We've been socialized to boast about running two miles, not walking two blocks. But some days we should applaud ourselves for just getting out of bed.

At any rate, I walked one block, then two, then the hill in front of my house, then a mile to a nearby school. I dug down into the depths of my being to muster the will to get stronger. One day while walking, I realized I was late for carpool and started running.

If you are going to change your attitude, you have to have a plan. You have to know exactly what behavior or condition you intend to modify and what steps you must take to do it. You must make your plan unique and tailored to you. You must focus on reasonable goals, baby steps to the final result—your ability to apply attitude therapy principles and have a great, positive attitude.

Don't Be Afraid to Dig Deep

When I was sick, my biggest downfall was not getting enough rest. I would continually fall into the trap of being all things to all people (a self-set trap, I might add). I had to make a plan. Making a plan required delving into the loneliness imposed by my illness, the place where I hid my fear of failing and my goal of getting better. I had to admit to myself that I was in denial about my illness.

Sticking my head in the sand was not all bad. I was very careful not to think about being sick, instead focusing on being well. When I was 18 and trying desperately to interrupt the viscous, self-defeating cycle of endless partying, I was in a similar state of denial and had to go to a very lonely place inside myself. The same will be true for you when you decide to quit playing games and get to work on your own personal goals.

Years later, when I was fighting for physical survival and worrying about a brain tumor, I faked being well and happy. I felt that my body had waged a war against me over which I had no control. Obviously, rest was an important part of getting better. So I knuckled down and went to work on that one goal.

I was carrying a lot of baggage, which is one of the reasons I faked it the best I could. I didn't want my husband to abandon me for someone else (which was *stinkin' thinkin'*, by the way). My fear motivated me to be a full participant in our life together, despite my illness, thus turning a negative into a positive driving force.

I faked it a lot because of my children and the extreme stress they experienced watching me have seizure after seizure until we found a medication that worked. A couple of years ago, while boarding a plane, my little daughter, Molly, looked at me and began to cry and reach for her big brother. When I asked what was wrong, she sobbed that she didn't want me to fall down in the airport and act crazy, as I had once before. The stress and strain affected my entire family. When one person in a family is sick, everyone is sick.

Start Small and Simple

Begin by setting a couple of small, short-term goals specific to your needs. This will help you to build confidence. Sometimes a small change can make a world of difference in your attitude.

I once consulted with a physician to improve the efficiency and organization of his office. In the process, I learned that his wife phoned him several times a day with requests and reminders. Invariably she would ask him to stop at the market on the way home and purchase milk or some other needed item. My client resented both the interruptions and having to do grocery shopping at the end of each long, tiring day. His wife was not employed outside the home and had her own car. Clearly, inefficiencies at home were exacerbating those at work. After considerable discussion, the doctor set a goal: to tell his wife in a few plain, assertive words that both the phone calls and the errands had to stop. This was not easy for him to do, but he somehow managed. At a later meeting, when my client's resentment toward his wife had largely subsided, I encouraged him to set another goal. This time he was to identify things he liked about his wife—things that made him happy—and communicate those to her on a regular basis. The aim of this second goal was to replace a negative attitude with a positive attitude—to replace resentment with appreciation.

We often set goals aimed at changing negative behaviors. This is fine as long as the goals themselves are not negative. Reducing or eliminating a bad habit—smoking, overeating, procrastinating, gossiping or swearing—is not a sufficient goal.

The most effective way to break a habit is to substitute a new behavior and practice it until it becomes routine. A reforming smoker takes walks during breaks previously devoted to smoking. A distracted driver substitutes classical music for cell-phone conversations on the road. This approach is especially helpful when setting attitude-related goals. If your goal is to stop an undesirable behavior—complaining, blaming, procrastinating, avoiding—be sure to substitute a desirable behavior for the one you are trying to eliminate. Then focus on the positive side of the equation. Concentrate on building, not destroying.

Here's another reason to limit your goals and keep them simple: goals are no picnic to achieve. On paper, they may look easy, just as diets look easy. But even the simplest diet is extremely difficult—impossible for some people. Why? Because changing a behavior requires vigilance and willpower—and willpower in turn requires passion and commitment.

Set Clear, Concise Goals

Finding your passion requires that you think about what you really want from life and then start moving in the right direction. Yesterdays don't matter. Tomorrow is uncertain. *Now* is where you must focus.

You *can* change, but first you must have the desire and a clear, concise goal. In Chapter 2, I suggested that you examine your attitude in a number of areas and pinpoint specific changes that you would like to make. If you completed the Data Dump exercise, you've uncovered additional valuable information.

In this chapter, I want you to set some specific goals. For example, perhaps you've discovered that your inability to sustain an exercise program is related to a defeatist attitude about exercise. (It is for many people.) You approach exercise as if it were punishment and frequently tell yourself and others how much you despise it. That attitude might get you around the block for a few days, but pretty soon you'll find some excuse to quit. So setting an exercise goal won't do much good unless you set a related attitude goal. What should be your attitude toward exercise? Well, that depends. Transforming loathing and dread to joyful anticipation in one stroke is asking too much, so develop a more modest goal. Depending on your personality and disposition, you might decide to approach exercise with an attitude of curiosity, or one of patience, or one of quiet determination.

A curious attitude would inspire you learn about the benefits of exercise, read some of the research, experiment with different forms of exercise to determine what best suits you, and try a variety of venues, such as classes, health spas and walking clubs. With a patient attitude, you would probably take it slow and be very accepting of your body's aches, pains and general lethargy. You would not scold yourself or feel defeated, you would take a long-range view and move steadily in that direction. A determined attitude would utilize self-discipline, strict adherence to an exercise schedule, and zero tolerance for excuses. Whichever mindset you chose, the goal would be to substitute the new attitude of curiosity, patience, or determination (or a combination) for the old attitude of loathing and dread. When old defeatist feelings rekindled, you would deliberately and soundly douse them with feelings generated by the new attitude.

Break Down Complicated Goals

Your attitude must allow you to tackle a problem and break it down into manageable pieces. I tell all of my students to address each challenge bit by bit. If you were going to write a paper for a college course, the professor would give you the instructions well in advance, so that the research and writing could be done over an extended period of time. Last minute cramming might get the job done, but the results would be less than ideal.

If you were to start a crash diet today, using pills, supplements and any other crutch you could find, you might lose 30 pounds in as little as three months, but how long would it stay off? Long-term weight loss must be a life-altering experience, involving a complete change of lifestyle. New food habits (not just eating habits, but shopping, cooking, snacking and dining-out habits) must be adopted for weight loss to be truly successful and long term. Positive thinking works exactly the same way. You must slowly develop life-changing habits that will stay with you and be there when you need them. Furthermore, if maintaining a good attitude is part of your daily agenda, you will generate an environment conducive to growth and development during both the good times and the bad.

A relatively sedentary lifestyle during my long period of illness caused me to gain a good deal of weight. So, in addition to running, I borrowed a Weight Watcher's "points book" from a friend and immediately began calculating food values. I listed the days of the week on a sheet of paper and added columns for recording the foods I ate, their point value and amounts of daily exercise. Keeping records seemed like a good idea, so I upped the ante and began planning my meals in advance. Every Sunday night for weeks I wrote out Monday's menu, making sure I ended up with the correct number of points for my target weight. Weight Watchers allows people extra points for exercise—not me. Determined and with tunnel vision I pressed on. It took me about five months to lose 43 pounds and keep it off.

All those lists and calculations related to my weight-loss goal served a dual purpose. Not only were they tantamount to a series of small steps, those steps kept me very busy. I always felt as though I was doing something productive to reach the goal. The feeling of productiveness helped to fuel further efforts, so the approach was intrinsically motivating.

Anticipate and Prepare for Problems

Play your cards close to your vest until you experience some success with your plan. Then share it with others. Step out in confidence and live your plan openly.

At first, many conflicting thoughts will work against you. One day you may have your negative thoughts under control, and the next day those little demons will raise their ugly heads again. Keep fighting. Keep an outline in your plan close by. It may not be a business plan, but it *is* a serious business.

A good plan will anticipate problems and spell out ways of overcoming them. If you have this, the only thing you need to implement it is willpower. Lots and lots of willpower.

Make checklists of the daily steps you need to take to work your plan and maintain positive thinking. Your checklist could be as simple as: 1. Get up (Check!); 2. Get dressed (Check!); 3. Walk to the car (Check!); 4. Drive to work (Check!).

Take baby steps. Develop a cadence specific to your needs.

Visualize Success

In his book, *The Magic of Believing*, Claude M. Bristol writes that we need to create a mental picture of what we want and keep telling ourselves that we are going to achieve our goals. "But don't think it is going to come to you if you merely indulge in a period of watchful waiting," he cautions. Get to work and start moving the process forward.

A common problem confronting many people is the lack of money, but according to Bristol, capital can be attracted by thought. He points out that many wealthy people in the investment banking business are "money conscious." Their repetitive thoughts about wealth make coming to possess it a natural process.

Entrepreneurs with workable ideas rarely have difficulty in financing their endeavors. However, Bristol cautions that entrepreneurs must be thoroughly convinced their ideas will work before they can convince others to lend them money.

You have to have a clear image of what you desire in order to realize your goal. Through repetition, the goal is deeply embedded in the subconscious mind. Realization of the goal is gradually achieved because all of your senses and powers become devoted to that conclusion.

For example, if you want a particular promotion, you have to tell yourself, and continuously visualize, that you are getting that job. The repetition will drive the idea deeply and firmly into your subconscious. The subconscious will accept and, in turn, carry out whatever it is powerfully instructed to do.

Bristol suggests that you imagine your mind as a room with only one door. You have the key. It's your job to decide who or what is allowed through the door—whether you are subjected to positive or negative thoughts, and which ones to let in.

Simply put, your subconscious responds to your strongest sensations. Urges Bristol, "You must at all times keep your mind filled with positive thoughts so that their strong vibrations will ward off all negative and destructive thoughts that might come from the outside."

Courageously Pursue Your Plan

Life is full of ups and downs, but when you are in the midst of pain and fear, try to believe that good things are right around the corner. That is the paradox of life. At times we are on the mountaintops and at times we are in the valleys. It can't be any other way.

Rather than taking a negative view of this truth, prepare yourself for the down times by developing a positive attitude. Have a plan *before* you tumble into a valley. Be ready—or as ready as one can be. No harm can come from acknowledging in advance the certainty of hard times and having your plan in place.

Identify exactly where you need to improve, what attitude needs to be adjusted, and how you will get there from here. Make a plan and go forward. Struggle, fall down beneath the load, but get up and keep working the plan, exercising strong willpower. If determination and willpower don't come naturally, learn them, just as you would learn any new skill. Anything you learn comes with rules. Attitude is no different. The rules are not easy, so take bite-size pieces. Make up your mind about what you are going to do in particular areas of your life—career, marriage, family, wellness. Then forge ahead and chase your dreams.

Exercise #5

To-Be Lists

Most people are practiced at making to-do lists. In this exercise, you will create a *to-be* list. As a child, you probably made declarations such as, "I want to be a fireman when I grow up" or "I want to be the cowboy (bad guy, Indian, princess, etc.) Now, as an adult, step back and make some conscious decisions about the person you want to be.

Objectives:

This exercise will assist you to:

- Clarify the kind of person you want to be.

- List desirable qualities and characteristics to which you aspire.

Materials:

Paper and pencil or computer

Time required:

Approximately 30 minutes

Procedure:

1. Spend a few minutes envisioning the person you would like to be. Include physical qualities (appearance, health and fitness), mental qualities (education, skills, problem-solving ability), emotional qualities (feelings, attitudes), character qualities (ethics, values), and spiritual qualities (faith, religious practice).

2. Create a separate list for each category. Begin each statement with: I want to be …and fill in the blank. Write until you can no longer think of additional qualities; however, do not list qualities because you think you "ought to" or "should." List only qualities to which you sincerely, deeply aspire.

3. Prioritize the final list, or simply circle the qualities that are most important to you.

4. Develop a specific goal and plan for each of the three top qualities.

STOP

Think about what you have learned from this chapter. Review your reactions and decide how you will use this information.

6

A Checkup from the Neck Up

A Lupus patient can require hospitalization during bouts with the common cold. I was hospitalized numerous times for pneumonia and dehydration due to long periods of vomiting and diarrhea. Arthritis in my jaw caused my mouth to freeze open after sneezing. My jaw had to be manipulated closed, and I was given high doses of morphine for the pain. I was hospitalized for strep throat. I have had cortisone injections in every part of my anatomy for arthritis, bursitis and plain old "meanitis!"

Lupus is sometimes referred to as the "body against itself," and I can attest to the fact that my body waged war for many, many years. Life from ages 24 to 47 was a blur and largely wasted. I have been told that my struggles are an inspiration to many people. To me this is an enlightening and humbling insight.

Everything you need to enjoy a fulfilling life resides above your shoulders and between your ears. Regardless of your individual circumstances—your relative wealth, health, beauty and youth—happiness is a knack that can be developed by you or anyone. Happiness is a habit, an act of will.

We can learn a lot from athletes. Athletes become great through training and dedication. Fans watch in awe as they persevere through enormous challenges. Vince Lombardi once said, "The difference between a successful person and others is not a lack of strength, not a lack of knowledge, but rather a lack of will." We have to train our minds to be determined and motivated. It is not always the fastest person who wins the race, but rather the person who puts the most into the race.

Many of us blame our attitudes on other people or outside circumstances. It is easy to say, "She made me react that way," or "He ruined my day." It's humbling, but much more productive to acknowledge your own culpability. When you blame people or circumstances outside yourself, you relinquish power. When you accept responsibility for your choices (attitude is a choice), you reclaim power. A helpless victim is by definition incapable of changing anything. So if you want to change your attitude, you have to start by accepting responsibility. You authored your attitude—your signature is written all over it. Vow that you will no longer blame others for who you allow yourself to be.

Start Each Day with a Checkup

When you wake up in the morning, take an immediate inventory of your thoughts. Do a "checkup from the neck up." Ask yourself questions about where you are in your search for happiness. What is within your control to change? How can you become a happier person?

Imagine waking up daily with a broken leg. Wouldn't you ask yourself how your leg was feeling that day, if it had the degree of mobility that the doctor was hoping for, and if you should stretch and work the leg more or less? If you had pneumonia, wouldn't you check to see if you were breathing more easily and wonder about the results of the previous day's chest x-rays? So why not wake up and do a check of your mental attitude? Why not decide which features of your disposition you will work on this day and imagine yourself thinking and responding differently.

As part of your wakeup routine, close your eyes and visualize how you will interact with people and respond to events throughout the day. If you have an early morning meeting scheduled, see yourself entering the room and greeting everyone enthusiastically. If you've been having conflicts with a particular coworker, visualize a day of congenial collaboration. Many athletes use visualization to improve performance. While lying in bed, they visualize shooting hoops, running marathons, putting perfectly, or acing tennis serves. The more detailed the visualization, the more senses involved, the better. For example, hear the ball bounce, smell the leather, feel your grip on the ball before you shoot, and hear the *whoosh* as you watch the ball pass through the hoop. The benefits of visualization are well documented. Visualizing is a form of mental rehearsal. Actors rehearse their lines, singers rehearse their songs, football players rehearse specific plays, and you can rehearse your attitude.

Vary Your Routine

Another thing that can greatly affect attitude is boredom. Life can become a treadmill of monotonous routine. At work we go from one deadline to the next, one meeting to the next, one crisis to the next. As parents we go from one practice to the next, one homework assignment to the next, one car pool to the next. If your "treadmill" leaves you feeling dismal, frustrated and stressed, stop and do a "check up from the neck up." Ask yourself what you could do differently. I liken it to re-organizing the living room. First, observe the room and make mental notes. Second, take everything out. Third, put back only what you want to keep. Fourth, add new purchases. Fifth, take the old stuff to the attic.

Follow the same process with your daily routine. Take a time-out. Isolate and mentally line up all the elements of your schedule. Examine each one the way you would a suit that you've had for several years. Does it still fit? Does it still make you happy? Does it earn the respect of observers? Does it get the job done? Nothing in your routine should be considered sacred, because even essential things can be done in new and better ways. Once you've decided what to keep, reconfigure the pieces in a manner that pleases you. Take all the parts of your old routine that didn't make the cut and dispose of them one by one in a responsible manner. If other people are involved, call them up and explain the change. For example, if you no longer intend to participate in Friday TGIF parties, tell your friends that it was lots of fun, but you've decided to do something else instead. If you leave things dangling they will come back to haunt you, and the objective is to create satisfaction, not more problems.

It's a shame when we have to rely for excitement on increasingly violent movies and TV, outrageous celebrity conduct, venomous gossip and foolhardy physical exploits. Life is not a *Survivor* episode. Unless you are blind, deaf or otherwise afflicted, you have the capacity to be thrilled by a beautiful sunset, delighted by the voice of a child, amused by the antics of playful pets, and filled with joy when you contribute in some small way to the happiness of another. Like just about everything else, the relative vitality of your five senses is your responsibility. You can sleepwalk through life, feeling bored and unengaged, or you can open your eyes and ears to the wonders that surround you.

Get off the treadmill. *Things get better when you get better.*

Change Your Thinking

A bad attitude can grow and cause debilitating anger and heartache. Carrying emotional pain and *stinkin' thinkin'* can literally produce aching in the shoulders, back pain and other maladies. If you suffer from common "state of mind" depression (not medically diagnosed clinical depression), you can improve by exercising Attitude Therapy principles.

Depression is as much a disease as cancer, lupus or heart disease. However, just as patients with brain tumors, breast cancer, and lymphoma must work to maximize their treatment benefits, you must focus on your mental state. You must change your thinking, take control of your actions and respond to the attack on your life!

One of the most effective ways to change your emotional response to a situation is to change your thoughts about it. When another driver cuts you off at the freeway exit ramp, you have a choice. You can emit a barrage of epithets as you fight for your rightful place in the cue, or you can think, "He must be running late the morning," and yield. The first response will produce rancor, rapid pulse and a rise in blood pressure, and the second will foster nothing worse than mild disapproval. Does the other driver create your feelings? No, you do—with nothing more than your thoughts.

At the family dinner table, you can complain about your child's finicky eating habits, your teenager's unorthodox attire and your spouse's extra large helpings, or you can find something positive to say about each one, ignoring the rest. The complaints will be accompanied by feelings of dissatisfaction and self-righteousness, and the positive comments will produce warmth and pleasure. Does your family make these choices? No, you do.

When a conflict at work strains relationships, the tension and bitterness can affect many people, not just those who are party to the conflict. The longer ill feelings persist, the more antagonistic they grow. But regardless of who wins or loses, if you can find meaning in the conflict—if you can learn a lesson that will benefit you in future dealings—the tension will lift and the bitterness will transform into acceptance and appreciation.

If you are feeling depressed, you can exercise physically to make yourself tired so that you sleep better and feel replenished the next day. If you feel angry, simply cleaning up your thought processes may help. Pull out the negative thoughts as you would weeds in a garden. Decide who you want to be and how you want to impact others. After all, *you* are in control of your mindset and attitudes.

I've seen miracles occur simply by making people aware of their own actions or the way they are responding to crisis. They change their attitude toward their dilemma and *presto*, things turn around. You've heard the expression, "It's not what you say, but how you say it." Well, this is, "It's not what happens to you, but how you respond to what happens to you." Things get better when *you* get better. Change your thinking and get better.

Feeling Normal

As an Attitude Therapy consultant I'm often contacted when all hope is gone, when depression and fear have taken over. If a relative retains me, the patient usually is not quite as receptive to my presence as are family members. (I get the same reaction when an employer hires me to consult with organizational staff—the employees are not particularly excited about my intervention.)

When I come into a situation, the patient is usually sore and achy from being in bed for so long. I tell the patient that the first thing "we" are going to do is get up to take a shower. After we clean up, we are going to try to eat half a bagel—if we can get it down. Next, we are going to drive to Kroger or Kmart and get behind a shopping cart and push it around a little bit. The patient is usually mad at me, mad at the doctor, mad at life and mad at God, and protests, "You don't understand. I'm too tired, too weak, too sick, too scared, too, too, too…. However, I don't back down. I want the patient to become physically tired, a first step to gaining greater physical and mental fitness.

I encourage the patient to speak to a few people while we are out visiting the store. Then we get in the car and head back home. The patient takes a shower and crawls into a freshly made bed. The room has been tidied up and a couple of carnations or daisies have been placed in a small container by the bed.

Next, all of that "stuff" that sits by the bed—the wipes, tucks, medications, alcohol pads, swabs, Band-Aids®, and miscellaneous paraphernalia—gets tucked away in a big plastic container that slides neatly under the bed so the patient doesn't have to see it.

Everything you see, everything you perceive through your five senses, contributes to the way you feel. The brain is like the computer. Whatever goes into the computer comes out. If patients are constantly looking at all of the baggage that goes with being a home-bound sick person, they *become* that person. But if patients look at a floral arrangement sitting there, a nice clean pitcher with a sparkling glass turned upside down on a pretty towel so that when they feel thirsty they can pour some of that refreshing water, they feel better about life.

It might sound corny, but if trash goes into your computer, trash comes out. And quite frankly, I think that all of those supplies that go with being sick are trash. You need them, you've got to have them, but you don't have to look at them all day, and the room doesn't have to be in turmoil. You can look at other, nicer images of life. The room can be straightened up and the stink aired out. Sick people smell bad, largely because we don't clean them up. We don't want to make them tired, or fear they will become annoyed. Trust me, nobody likes to smell. And nobody likes to *smell* that smell.

If you are the patient, I promise you that in the first two days that I come to visit, we will do this attitude talking, and we will take our trip down to the local Kroger or Rite-Aid and get behind a shopping cart and walk a little bit, no matter how tired and shaky you are. I will tell you that I cannot extend your life. I don't have any magic, but I can make your life more enjoyable. And I can make you begin to see some important things in your life that you haven't thought about for a long time. I will ask you questions that will provoke your mind and memory to produce positive thoughts.

In my experience, by the fifth day, you will be feeling much better. This improvement comes from seeing people, getting out, and from the release of endorphins through exercise and contact with the real world. By day 10, you will be ready to discuss your attitude, the problems you are facing and some possible solutions. At this point, we will start goal setting.

If you have only two years left, how are you going to live those years? You need to develop a plan, decide what things you want to accomplish and how you want to act. In other words, make choices. Don't just kick back and give up. Don't let the cancer (or whatever) push you around or determine how you will go through your final days.

Granted, I cannot extend life, but I *can* make life a little more enjoyable and a bit more normal. People like to be normal, whatever they perceive that to be. I get them up and start cleaning them up and walking them around, and they begin to feel like people. Our activities and conversations make them feel like there's something more to life than their illness.

In her book, *There's No Place Like Hope*, Vickie Girard writes that, "The only people who can be assured of death from cancer are those who choose not to fight." After being diagnosed with Stage Four cancer, Girard decided to battle the disease. Instead of getting her affairs in order and waiting to die, she survived and became an advocate for patient empowerment .

"The thought of dying from cancer scares everyone, that is a given, but that's not the sad part. What is sad is that the fear sometimes causes people to give up their lives without a fight. I've met patients who are already gone in their minds—they are just waiting for their body to catch up. I want to shake them, for they are throwing away exactly what they are so afraid of losing," she writes.

Grave illness is not an automatic death sentence. You have to decide to face the battle and find purpose and meaning in life.

Keeping the End in Sight

I teach participants in my Attitude Therapy classes to write obituaries, first as they would read today, and then as participants wish them to read. It takes effort to make the re-written obituary a reality when it is finally needed.

Chronic sufferers and terminally ill people have something folks who die suddenly aren't afforded. In many cases they have time to get their affairs in order—to plan, make changes, reach goals and prepare.

Years ago, my friend, Shirley, lost her husband following a lengthy battle with cancer. Not too long afterward, Shirley found herself fighting the same disease. Although she managed to survive long enough to raise her twin boys, her health eventually worsened.

I received a phone call from Shirley on a Sunday morning before church and went to visit her in the hospital. She calmly asked me, "Do you think it is okay if I die now? I am tired … so tired." I looked at her and said, "Yes, Shirley, I think it will be fine."

Shirley had reached a milestone. Her sons were heading off to college in the fall and she felt as though it was time to end her fight. I thought about this for a minute and then said, "Shirley, you don't have to die. If we work hard, I think we can get you through this."

But Shirley explained that she was just too tired to continue and had made her decision. She passed away a short time later.

We are always trying to control things—external things—and often don't realize that the one thing we do control is our mind. Be determined to take control of your mind and your life. Become absorbed in "getting better." Life is short. Don't go through life upset, grumpy, and just barely existing. You can do anything if you set your mind to it—anything!

Exercise #6

Write Your Eulogy or Obituary

Objectives

The purpose of this exercise is to understand how others perceive you, evaluate how closely their views match your ideal image of yourself, and determine where you wish to make changes.

Materials

Writing materials or computer

Time required

Approximately 1 hour

Procedure

1. Pretend that it is many years from now. A dear friend is standing at the podium in front of the guests at your memorial service or funeral, about to deliver a eulogy. Write the eulogy that you would like your friend to deliver. As an alternative, write the obituary that will appear in the local newspaper. How do you want the eulogy or obituary to describe you? What qualities and accomplishments do you want it to list? What is the legacy for which you hope to be remembered?

2. Now repeat the exercise, but this time pretend that today is the last day of your life. Write what your eulogy or obituary would say if it were written today.

3. Compare the two eulogies or obituaries. Identify the things that you need to change or accomplish in order to become the person that you want loved ones to remember after you are gone.

4. Begin today to set goals and develop action plans aimed at creating the person you want to be. This is the first day of the rest of your life.

STOP

Think about what you have learned from this chapter. Review your reactions and decide how you will use this information.

7

Time on Task

The Reverend Esber Tweel has been quite close to death in recent months. On Ash Wednesday, 2006, he sat in church feeling the erratic pounding of his heart and thought, "Hey, I've just been absolved, God, so take me tonight before I can wake up and sin again." Later, on his way to the hospital he said aloud, "Okay, Lord, can't you take a damn joke?"

Rev. Tweel's body has been in decline for years from the disease polymyositis. His conflicting sentiments during and after the Ash Wednesday incident are typical of the merry-go-round of emotions that accompany his disease. One minute he feels like dying, the next he's working hard to live.

The disease, which causes atrophy of muscles and the eventual loss of the ability to breathe, has been devastating to the reverend, particularly since he is an avid practitioner of the martial arts. He still practices the spiritual side of the arts, while rehearsing the movements in his mind. "In fact, I'm faster and more accurate than anyone!" he laughs. "In my mind I am stronger and more capable than I've ever been."

He says when people ask him how he's doing, he never says "better." He says he's "different," because to say better would be inaccurate. He has come to terms with how his body is right now. That realization has allowed the reverend to keep a positive attitude—to joke and laugh with God. "I could handle this with hurt, anger and dismay, or I can approach it with peace, harmony and love. Which will make me stronger?"

It is important that you decide how you are going to be in life. You need to spend as much time on your attitude, rehearsing your role in life, as you would practicing lines for a play. If you were to take up tennis or golf, you would spend a great deal of time on your lessons. You would work to perfect your forehand or improve your putting ability. If you decided to study voice or piano, you would go to a lesson, then practice, then go back for another lesson.

Most people never give a second thought to their attitude until a crisis occurs in their life. They don't try to get better until something of great magnitude walks up and hits them right between the eyes and sends them reeling. My goal is to prepare the people I teach and coach to go out and face each day with a better attitude, come what may. When difficult circumstances walk into their lives, as they most certainly will, they will be better equipped to handle them by having an improved mental outlook as a result of this preparation and planning.

This is what I mean by "time of task." I'm sold on the concept. Many times I can be heard giving my husband a hard time with statements like, "Don, your tennis game is awesome! Time on task!" or "Don, your listening skills stink. Time on task!" I regularly compliment my children on their achievements, reinforcing the notion that time devoted to any worthy pursuit pays big dividends.

A Little Is Not Enough

To change a behavior, you have to spend time on task. For example, if your goal is to modify a quick temper, there's work to do—tangible work, like anger management classes. It's not enough to occasionally mention that you are trying to control your temper, as if recognizing the problem is all it takes. Awareness is a start, certainly, but without action it's just lip service. You can talk about your intentions "'til the cows come home," but to realize improvement you have to spend time on task.

An occasional effort isn't sufficient either. In the July 23, 2006, issue of *Parade* magazine, a reader asked columnist Marilyn vos Savant if an occasional vitamin is enough to produce better health, and if occasionally parking your car in the garage is enough to make a difference in the condition of its body. Her answer? No. She explained that the difference in behavior has to be enough to matter in some way, because doing anything (taking a vitamin or parking the car) uses time, an extremely valuable resource. She stated, "Too many people spend time and money pursuing lots of goals just a little."

Imagine trying to become skillful at tennis, golf, running, basketball and swimming all at the same time. How much progress could you make in any one sport if you divided limited practice time among five different disciplines? The answer, obviously, is very little. Attitude is no different. If you are trying to accomplish so many different things that you give only intermittent attention to your attitude, nothing will change. You've got to spend time on task.

A Five-Step Process

Below is a brief outline of my recommended five-step process. I'm going to elaborate on the temper example, but you can and should apply these steps to whatever behavior you are attempting to change.

Step one: Think about why you have a quick temper and what seems to set it off. Get a good understanding of the behavior you are trying to correct. Don't try to rationalize your behavior. Just think back over recent weeks or months and objectively record the instigator of each temper outburst. This is data gathering, nothing more.

Step two: Go to the Internet, the library, or a bookstore and search for information on temper, anger, emotional intelligence and other related subjects. Load up with reference materials and read, read, read.

Step three: Repeat step one, using this newly acquired information to enlarge your understanding of your own combative behavior. Allow a minimum of several days to mull over everything you've pieced together. Record insights as notes or journal entries.

Step four: Write a plan for improvement. Set a precise goal and develop action steps leading to the goal. For example, the goal might be to reduce temper flare-ups by eighty percent, and the steps might include taking an anger management class, practicing specific control techniques, and cutting down on caffeine and alcohol.

Step five: Review your progress and self-correct on a regular basis. Do this for several months. If something comes up that you don't understand or can't deal with, go back to the Internet for more information, or consult an expert.

You can't just wake up one morning and decide to be a more positive person. It requires a lot of practice, deliberation, determination and dedication. You must practice the art and be invested in it like you would an exciting career, a favorite hobby, or a new romance. In order to get results, you have to practice, practice, practice!

Time on task pays off! Would you sign on as captain of a ship if you had no experience? Would you fly a plane without a pilot's license and the appropriate number of hours in the air? The most important asset you have is the very thing you must now take charge of—your life! You must practice and prepare to better your best.

Think of a runner, a tennis player, or a new person on the job. How many of these people start right out at the top of their game without any practice or training? How many exceptional golfers do you know who never practice? Do you think you could go out today and run 10 miles, never having trained? Or win a tennis match with no knowledge of the game? Practice makes perfect! Time on task—any task—will bring you to a new level of success.

Twenty-one Days

I rarely see people deliberately attempting to develop attitude skills. I don't see them behaving as though they realize that what happens to them is not as important as how they respond to what happens to them. So I am challenging you to begin to practice having a good attitude—to experience an attitude adjustment.

Being diagnosed with lung cancer would give you an opportunity to change your lifestyle. It would not be easy and you would need a plan. The plan would have to be charted, monitored, checked and re-checked. If you were told that your heart was failing and that you had to change your eating and exercise habits, you would need to create and implement a very specific plan. According to the American Heart Association, today's minimum exercise requirement for a healthy heart is 30 minutes of exercise most days of the week, 60 minutes if you are trying to lose weight. Healthful habits take about 21 days to form, so it's not as simple as saying, okay, I'll start exercising. Habits are built over time with repetition. If 21 days seems like a long time to you, just remember that the rewards are ongoing—they last forever.

For Karin, attitude practice began years ago, when she was a child. Now 36, Karin has experienced total renal failure, three kidney transplants, a heart attack, and a triple bypass to relieve blockages caused by years of dialysis, starting when she was only 15. When she was first diagnosed with kidney disease at age seven, her mother told her that chronic renal failure was not reversible—there was no cure—so Karin had a choice. She could be miserable and unhappy, which would probably make her illness worse, or she could be optimistic and strong, which was bound to make her feel better. Karin internalized that message and put it to daily practice growing up. Today, with her third transplanted kidney working well, Karin is an attractive, busy woman with a supportive fiancé and a terrific outlook. Time on task is *exactly* what produced her amazingly resilient attitude.

Unlike Karin, most of us can practice our positive attitudes during neutral periods, so that we are ready to apply them to whatever horrible events march into our lives. I don't want to be negative, just realistic. Bad things happen. They don't present themselves in order of magnitude, with event A more easily handled than event B, and event B preparing us for event C. They enter our lives in random order. Every day I work with folks who have experienced terrible shock and pain in their lives, and it just breaks my heart. Some have lost a child to drugs or in an automobile accident.

Gloria went shopping one day and came home to find a half dozen of her closest friends waiting for her. The small plane that her husband piloted that day had crashed and burned shortly after takeoff. Her friends were there to break the news. Tenacious and bright, Gloria had every conceivable character quality at her advantage, but nothing, absolutely nothing could have prepared her for that moment.

You get up in the morning and go shopping and come home to find your life completely, irrevocably changed. That's how it happens. And that, dear reader, is why time on task is so important.

Basic Training

Once, while watching Good Morning America in an airport lounge, I observed the hosts interview a health specialist. They were discussing breast cancer and a woman's need to get involved and fight back spiritually, intellectually, and physically. The guest reviewed the benefits of exercise and staying trim. They discussed the role of fighter cells that kick in to attack the enemy cancer cells waging war on the body.

Like a trained army, physical, emotional and spiritual "fighter cells" must be on standby, ready to mobilize and go to war. We must prepare ourselves to fight back *prior* to the disease attacking. We need to keep our army fit and in shape should a crisis occur. Women need to be coached and mentored to stay healthy and fit. I am not just talking about dieting—there's plenty of that already. To be ready to battle divorce, the death of a loved one, or the illness of a child, we need to be "lean, mean fighting machines," and attitude plays a big part in this training. We need an "attitude show" on TV, with guests and "happy ending" stories that teach and foster good attitudes.

Singer Patti Labelle is known for her powerful voice and boundless energy, but many people do not know that she was diagnosed with diabetes more than a decade ago. Today she is a spokeswoman for early intervention. In infomercials urging at-risk people to test for diabetes, Labelle says, "I have diabetes. Diabetes doesn't have me." I love the way she phrases that comment. It reminds me that sometimes in life a slight attitude adjustment is all that's required.

Daily Treatment

Alcoholics abuse their minds and bodies, and their spirits as well. I learned a great deal about alcoholism while managing the temporary service. When a home for recovering alcoholics in my community asked me to place some of its residents in jobs, I attended several meetings to learn more about alcoholism. I vividly remember people in the group standing and saying, "You may not be responsible for this disease, but you damn well *are* responsible for your recovery."

I remember one man saying that he would be in therapy every day for the rest of his life. "I get up in the morning and thank God that he kept me from drinking throughout the night, because I used to drink all night." He went on to say that people are not responsible for having diabetes or arthritis or most other chronic diseases. "I used to think that all diseases were 'event' diseases. You have appendicitis, you cut it out. You have measles, you get over it. You have pneumonia, you take penicillin and get well. Now I realize that some diseases have to be treated every day."

Obstacles may keep you from living a full life, but it's up to you to turn those obstacles into challenges and blast through the negativity to find solutions. Like alcoholism, negative thinking is a disease. And like alcoholism, it must be treated every day.

Exercise #7

21 Stories

I have included 21 brief stories in the back of this book to encourage you to improve your attitude, develop empathy, and attain your goals in life. It takes 21 days to form an habit. Use these stories to develop the habit of approaching life with a positive attitude.

Objective:

This exercise is designed to help you:
- Develop empathy.
- Recognize that maybe you don't have it so bad after all.
- Develop an attitude of hopefulness and gratitude.

Materials:

This book, nothing more

Time required:

Ten minutes a day for 21 days

Procedure:

1. Each day for 21 consecutive days, read a different story from the back of this book. Each story describes the experiences of a real person. No last names have been used, but the first names and photographs are real.

2. As you read the story, imagine what it would be like to *be* that person. In your imagination, walk in his or her shoes.

3. If your own troubles are worse than those of the person whose story you read, take courage from this person's positive outlook, knowing that you, too, can overcome.

4. When you have finished reading the story, take a few moments to be grateful for the blessings in your own life, and silently vow to demonstrate respect and appreciation for them throughout the day.

STOP

Think about what you have learned from this chapter. Review your reactions and decide how you will use this information.

8

Developing Empathy

I am thankful for my trials and tribulations. I would not be the person I am today if it weren't for the pain. I would not have focused on being well—on exercise, eating right, smelling the roses.

I cling to every moment, every milestone in the lives of my children. I savor the tender moments. I am humbled by the simple things of life. I look at life differently after being diagnosed with a brain tumor and having many years of seizures. I confront the hassles by asking: would I rather be late for work, or have a brain tumor? Would I rather have the flu, or a brain tumor?

...a flooded basement, or a brain tumor?
...a canceled flight, or a brain tumor?
...a missed sale, or a brain tumor?
...shin splints, or a brain tumor?
...lost tennis match, or a brain tumor?
...sick kids, or a brain tumor?

As a society we are in such a hurry, with so much to do and so little time in which to do it, we strike out at others almost reflexively. A typical day at Wal-Mart, Target or Kroger finds people rushing up to sales counters and confronting sales clerks in the most demanding tones. We expect undivided attention and expert knowledge without giving a thought to what kind of day that clerk might be having. It could be the clerk's first day on the job. He or she might have a sick child at home. Do we empathize? No.

Applying the Golden Rule

Being quite driven myself—a controlled Type A—I understand what it's like to have an impatient, demanding temperament. In my opinion, we A's would do ourselves a great favor by examining the motives that spur uncontrolled, unkind behavior. We need to stop and ask ourselves, "Is this how I would like to be treated if I were that store clerk? Is walking all over people what life is all about? Who am I to behave so shabbily toward another human being?"

I feel that if any of us were to ask ourselves these questions, we would stop behaving like spoiled, self-important harpies. Not only would this pave the way to greater success in our individual lives, it would lower our blood pressure and reduce the odds of our having a heart attack.

On the other hand, if you are the store clerk and are ignoring customers while talking personal business on the telephone, you are robbing your employer of time, money and the good service needed to retain customers. You might ask yourself what behaviors would please customers and thereby generate greater sales. You might try doing something as simple as making eye contact with customers and showing genuine interest in helping them. Service and retail employees who are paid commissions for the actual job they do quickly become more focused—or they quit and find a different line of work.

I read someplace years ago about a study on personal phone calls in the workplace and how costly they are to companies. The average white-collar worker in the U.S. spent more than one hour a week talking on the phone to friends and family on company time. This was one of the principle findings of a nationwide survey commissioned by Accountemps, which found that white-collar workers made an average of 3.14 personal calls a day, with each conversation running slightly less than five minutes.

When I added it up, the total came to about 62 hours of personal phone conversations a year, or 11 days of "vacation" time that the company was paying for. Today, with emails and the Internet, the figures are much higher.

Before you speak or act, think about how your behavior will affect those around you. In something as simple as shopping, you could be the best thing that happens all day to a lot of different people. Just by controlling your attitude you could brighten instead of darken their day.

If we want to see what our children are going to be like when they grow older, all we have to do is look in the mirror. On certain days, that's a scary prospect, and not because of the way we look so much as the way we act. We go off half-cocked so often in life. We respond and react without thinking. Instead, we should plan and prepare by examining our thought processes and determining what sort of behavior will bring us happiness and peace of mind and what sort of example we want to set for our children.

Recently I observed the selfless act of a young male passenger who assisted an older lady onboard an airplane by taking her bag and placing it in the overhead compartment. Her face and eyes lit up with appreciation. As it turned out, she had been running to catch the plane. The airline had inadvertently announced the wrong departure gate, so people who were already running late (like this lady) were *really* late when they were told to go to D-26 instead of C-26. To make matters worse, she was traveling with two people in wheelchairs and her stress level was off the charts. The young man's simple act of kindness went a long way toward redeeming her day. Why did he do it? Perhaps it was the automatic response of a young person who had been repeatedly drilled throughout youth in the old-fashioned courtesies—opening doors and holding chairs and carrying bags. Or maybe he experienced a conscious moment of empathy, of looking at the woman and picturing himself, pressured, embarrassed and struggling in her place.

How Empathy Works

Empathy is getting inside another person's shoes and experiencing the situation from his or her perspective. It is being thrilled for a person when he triumphs. It is being sad for a person when she mourns. It is matching fear with fear, dread with dread, anger with anger, excitement with excitement. Empathy doesn't compete with or take away from what the other person is feeling. Empathy mirrors and supports it. Empathy is not the same thing as sympathy. It is much more complicated and much more potent.

The human brain seems to be wired for empathy. Researchers have filmed the responses of observers watching a person cope with an unusual predicament, such as attempting to balance a tall stack of packages while walking down a crowded sidewalk. The bodies of the observers mimic, or mirror, the attempts of the person to balance the load. Researchers believe that the brains of observers automatically produce mirroring movements in an effort to understand what the other person is experiencing.

If you watch fans at a football game, you will see them use their bodies to mimic passing and blocking movements, and they will sometimes shrink back protectively when their favorite players are tackled.

These are demonstrations of empathy, of a desire to understand what others are experiencing. This natural tendency, when developed and expressed intentionally, can facilitate communication, enhance relationships and help settle conflicts. Empathy is a very powerful response, and one of the hallmarks of a positive attitude. Empathy conveys genuine interest and compassion.

Listening Conveys Empathy

The most powerful way that you can express empathy is by listening. I don't mean merely closing your mouth and pretending to listen while you think about something else. I mean really listening and doing things to demonstrate that you understand what the speaker is saying. A lot of people call this "active listening," because it involves more than simply sitting there passively while the other person talks.

To listen actively takes effort. You have to clear your mind of unrelated thoughts, avoid interrupting, concentrate, and attempt to truly understand what the other person is saying and feeling. When you do these things, your facial expressions and body language convey that understanding. You automatically smile, frown, grimace and look surprised at appropriate times. Of course, if you *don't* understand, you won't be able to honestly express empathy. If the speaker says something that confuses you, you have to ask for clarification in order to understand. If the speaker describes an experience that is completely foreign to you, you can't produce empathy because you've never been through a similar experience. But that doesn't happen very often. Most of us have experienced heartache, illness, and the loss someone we love. Most of us know what it feels like to win something, love someone, have a terrible argument, and feel insecure. So we definitely have the capacity for empathy. What we may not have is the desire.

If you act bored when someone is talking to you, the person will know that you are not really interested. But your level of interest is not the fault of the person speaking, it comes from within. Smile at people—not a fake smile, but one that shows genuine interest. Don't take out your frustrations on people. Don't be grumpy and grouchy because of something that happened to you earlier in the day. That kind of carryover attitude ignores the individual in front of you. Share your troubles with your spouse, or your therapist, or your best friend—the person you normally confide in. Beyond that, keep them to yourself. Continuous grumbling and growling brings people down.

I'm for the simple, old-fashioned notion that you should pay attention to what you are saying and doing. If you do, you won't have your foot in your mouth all the time. Focus on doing things in a polite and courteous way, not saying the first thing that pops into your mind.

You have to want to be empathetic. It requires energy. If you are lazy, or completely self-centered, you may find it difficult to expend the effort. Another barrier is fear. Some people are afraid to express emotion. They control their emotions so tightly that they don't dare allow themselves to empathize with others, because they might lose control. They might feel pain themselves and perhaps even cry. Often such people come across as very cold. Most are just afraid.

A woman I know developed a rare disease that caused her feet to become enflamed and swell painfully in response to even mild heat. For over two years, the only people who knew about her illness were the many doctors she consulted and her family. Finally, because she was forever making excuses to avoid activities like dancing, shopping trips and hiking, she decided to tell her best friend. The friend sat quietly and listened. She asked three or four questions. But she did not express an ounce of empathy. In fact, her summary statement before they parted was something to the effect that, "Well, these things happen as we get older." At first, the woman was devastated. This illness had changed her life. It was painful, difficult to treat and impossible to cure. Her friend's dismissive reaction seemed callous. Later the woman realized that her friend was simply afraid to feel or express empathy.

Children Deserve Empathy, Too

Despite separating and eventually divorcing several years ago, a couple I know have found a way to rise above the challenge of rearing children while being divorced. It is not uncommon to see them all together in the same car, riding to soccer games and swim practices. The parents speak of their situation in very pragmatic yet caring terms.

"Our kids come first," the father says. "They have suffered enough. We want them to feel as though they can come to either of us with anything."

This father and mother have found a way to cut through the drama of divorce and focus on the needs of their children. They share custody, enjoy the holidays together and sit beside each other and cheer their children during activities.

They have deep empathy for their children. While many divorced parents drop their kids off at the other parent's home and pick them up when the weekend is over, these parents are hands-on. They communicate with each other, and if children have a problem they can go to either parent.

Here's some advice for divorced parents: Remember, your primary obligation is to your children and their upbringing. The interests of your children—not your ego—come first. Look around you. Most of the children from single-parent homes are deprived of one parent or the other at any given time. Children should feel the love of two parents. They derive different strengths from each parent's support, nurturing, guidance and perspective.

A good friend once told me the following story about a mother's department store Christmas adventure.

A woman took her five-year-old son shopping at a large department store. It was December 23 and she wanted him to see all the decorations, window displays, toys and Santa Claus. She pulled him by the hand, twice as fast as his little legs would comfortably move. When he began to fuss and cry, she scolded, "What is the matter with you? I brought you with me to get into the Christmas spirit. Santa doesn't bring toys to little crybabies."

His fussing continued as she tried to find some last-minute bargains. "I'm never going to take you shopping with me again if you don't stop that whimpering," she threatened.

Just then the woman noticed that her son's shoes were untied, and knelt down to tie them. While on her knees, she happened to look up. For the first time, she viewed the large department store as her son did. Gone were the baubles and beads, the presents, the gaily decorated display tables and the animated toys. All she could see was a maze of corridors full of giant, stovepipe legs and huge posteriors. Mountainous strangers with feet as big as skateboards were pushing and shoving, bumping and thumping, rushing and crushing. Rather than fun, the scene looked absolutely terrifying!

The mother decided to take her son home and silently vowed never to impose her version of a good time on him again. The world may look good through adult eyes, but to a child it can be a scary journey.

Empathy allows us to understand the experiences of others. At the same time, it helps us to appreciate what we have. I have included numerous stories in this book for three reasons. First, I want you to see how positive attitudes have helped other people through difficult times. Second, I want you to realize that no matter how bad your situation, it could be worse. Third, I want you to develop empathy, one of the essential ingredients of a positive attitude.

First Impressions

It's easy to be wrapped up in the day-to-day minutia of family life and work. Suddenly, you look around and you are too successful, too old or too desperate to care how you have interacted with the many people in your life.

Think about how you receive others. You size them up. You assess them. You make assumptions about them based on your assessment. If you are like most people, you sometimes judge people based on a quick visual impression instead of taking the time to get to know them as individuals.

Some of this is simply instinctive human behavior. As a thinking creature, you can't completely discount your intuitive senses, but I'll bet you have learned (most of us have) that people can be completely different from your first impression.

Recently I gave a commencement address on this topic to a class of graduating high school students. To give the graduates a perspective, I used the example of my showing up at the commencement in my suit, dressed to the nines. I had never met most, if any, of the attendees prior to my address. I was introduced as a businessperson who had received numerous awards and been recognized for developing a company that spanned seven states and employed 4,000 people. That led most of the graduates to make certain assumptions about me. They thought they knew me.

Before concluding my address, I talked a little about my personal history. During this time I noticed many of the graduates moving to the edge of their chairs and paying closer attention. Suddenly I was not merely a "suit" brought in to speak to them. As I explained my early childhood pain and difficult life experiences, the graduates were sizing me up in a completely new light. I have experienced this phenomenon many times. I bet you have, too.

I also am reminded of Sam Walton, founder of Wal-Mart. Mr. "Sam," as he was known, would have the executives who traveled with him dress in suits and precede his arrival at a local Wal-Mart.

Then Mr. Sam would arrive in jeans and short sleeves. He wanted to be sure local store mangers paid attention to everyone, not just those people who "looked" important.

We tend to examine people by standing back and assuming we know their story and their content. That can result in many missed opportunities. We may pass up an opportunity by immediately saying no to clients, prospective employees or current employees with great ideas. We just don't give them the opportunity to present their viewpoints.

Consider the typical office receptionist. We instruct the receptionist to greet visitors by smiling and offering coffee, tea or a soft drink. We expect the receptionist to provide guests with a comfortable place to wait and to keep them posted as to when their meetings or appointments will occur.

Then, when it's our turn, we open the office door, meet the guests face to face for the first time and quickly give them a once-over. We sit down and conduct our meetings without necessarily giving these guests our full attention. We arrive at conclusions based either on our pre-judgment of each guest's skills, or the interest, or lack of interest, we have in their presentation. Our knowledge of the guest is finite, and yet his or her experiences may be vast.

If asked to render an opinion within our chosen profession, we don't hesitate to research the subject completely before offering our thoughts. Yet we are quick to short-shrift our usual analytical selves to make these snap judgments.

You may be secure in your career, or just starting. Regardless, my advice is to become very aware of your own behavior toward others. Just as people enjoy doing business with successful people, they enjoy doing business with kind and respectful people. People who practice the Golden Rule.

Try it. You'll get the hang of it. It doesn't matter whether you are ready to retire or just beginning your career. It is never too late to slow down and take time to listen to others while simultaneously getting to know them.

Weighing the Odds

Another thing we sometimes prejudge is our own likelihood of success. We size up a task, decide that the odds are against us, conclude that it's not worth the effort and give up. We quit without really trying, which is a tragedy.

There can be wisdom in cutting your losses, but to quit prematurely out of fear or laziness is a terrible mistake. I've seen people give up on goals, relationships, and life itself when just a little more effort might have produced success.

I know a tennis coach whose philosophy is to never prejudge the ball, even when it barely drops over the net. He coaches, "Go for it!" He has proven repeatedly that if you assert yourself, you can get to the ball by standing on the other side of the net and barely stroking the ball.

He yells, "You can do it!" and, sure enough, on the fourth or fifth try you find yourself actually getting to the ball.

Exercise #8
Assertiveness Practice

I once attended a luncheon where the topic of abortion came up. A girl who had chosen to have an abortion was being negatively judged by the women at the table. When a friend asked me for my opinion, initially I tried to avoid the question. Then I said I didn't have an opinion. My friend reminded me that as a Christian I *should* have an opinion. Finally I explained that, because I am a Christian, I need to pray for the girl and her situation, not make judgments. My goal is to be more Christ-like and less carnal, and in so doing I need to stay focused, not jump in and criticize. I further explained that I have experienced abortion and pray that my three daughters never do, but that I need to remain open-minded, offering love and support to women who have abortions as a result of rape, health issues or other factors. As a society, we seem to place numeric values on sin. For example, a man cheating on his wife is Sin Number 10, while a lady talking on the phone about her neighbor is Sin Number 2. I don't think so.

Objectives

The purpose of this exercise is to practice expressing strong opinions honestly and clearly, without being judgmental, overly aggressive, or offensive to others.

Materials

Writing materials or computer

Time required

Approximately 20 minutes

Procedure

1. Sit down at your computer, or with pad and pencil. Think of a controversial subject about which you have strong opinions. Write it down.

2. Using a "stream of consciousness" approach, write down your feelings and opinions about the subject.

3. Decide how you can hold this opinion and even express it when appropriate, without imposing it on others.

4. Practice expressing your opinion in a positive manner. Before you enter into discussions about controversial subjects, ask yourself if what you are about to say will make you a better person while contributing something of value to other people. You can still have opinions. You can even back them up with research or scripture, but make it a habit to express your opinions in unhurtful, nonjudgmental ways.

STOP

Think about what you have learned from this chapter. Review your reactions and decide how you will use this information.

9

All the Right Moves

*I met Tom Boyd several years ago while working out
at a gym. Many times I've watched him use two walking
sticks to hoist himself out of his wheelchair and complete
one loop around the gym's indoor running path.*

*Tom, a civil engineer and a pilot, was within 12 miles
of his destination when his single-engine plane stalled
due to ice in the carburetor that choked off the fuel
supply. As the plane was going down, Tom managed to
reach and maintain a gliding speed of 60 to 70 miles per
hour and then crash-landed the plane as successfully as
he could. That was in 1994.*

*Tom sustained serious injuries, including a compression
fracture of the vertebrae. The number one thing that Tom
thought about after regaining consciousness was the
need to find someone who could get him back on his
feet. That is still his goal today, more than a dozen years
later.*

*Different physicians have tried different treatments
and, of course, he has had surgery. As recently as a
year ago, he was still telling me about resources he was*

looking into. He is determined to find a doctor, clinic or rehabilitation facility that will get him back on his feet.

Have you ever witnessed someone express a sentiment without demonstrating any of the body language or facial expressions you would expect to accompany the words? Probably the most common example is the person who scowls while insisting, "I'm fine." It makes you question the truth of the statement and wonder if the person believes it himself. Often, you can determine a person's mood and attitude before he or she speaks, just by looking for nonverbal clues. Are the eyes dull, twinkling or flashing? Is the walk bouncy, heavy or dragging? Are the facial muscles tense or relaxed? How you feel affects your countenance, and vise-versa.

Try the following experiment. Slouch down in your chair, sink you chin into your chest and make your face look sad and depressed. Now, in this position, feel happy and confident. Tough, isn't it? When you are happy, your body doesn't cave in, it expands and becomes more animated. So it's pretty difficult feel happy in a drooping, sagging position. Your body and mind are inseparable. Where one goes the other follows.

Now do the opposite. Sit straight in your chair. Pull your shoulders back and take a deep breath. Lift your chin slightly and curve your lips into a smile. How do you feel now? Probably a good deal closer to happiness and confidence than you did before.

Congruent Messages

People tell me all the time that I seem to have a great deal of energy. While on vacation at Hilton Head recently, I was working to fix up a little courtyard patio that needed some plants. I had known the person I was working with for all of 10 minutes, and had never had a conversation with her previously. She said to me, "You seem to be an extremely high energy person." Now, I am about as calm and relaxed at the beach as I am capable of being. I don't know if commenting on my energy was a compliment or not, but I wasn't surprised that she sized me up so quickly. A lot of people do. My energy evidently shows in the pace at which I move and talk. That's the power of nonverbal communication.

Much of what people see in you results from your behavior and body language. If you express satisfaction with an employee's performance with a grim look and a dismissive tone, the employee will be confused at best, highly skeptical at worst. If your tone of voice is overly casual and your eyes are averted when you assure your boss that a project is "going well," she probably will not be convinced.

We read nonverbal behavior to get clues to one another's mood and disposition. The ability to control and interpret body language is a basic communication skill. However, the importance of nonverbal behavior goes beyond communication. Standing straight creates feelings of strength and confidence. In the military, it is a demonstration of discipline. In ballet, it connotes both discipline and control. In yoga, standing straight serves as the threshold to numerous yogic postures. My point is that while feelings affect body language, producing smiles, frowns, skipping and slouching, the reverse is also true. One of the most effective ways to modify your attitude and outlook is to change your facial expression and bearing. Carry yourself like a dignitary and you will feel more dignified. Surprise everyone by skipping around the office and see how quickly everyone, including you, starts laughing. Smile at the people you pass on the sidewalk or walking path and many of them will smile back, raising your spirits.

Benefits to the Immune System

In his book, *Anatomy of an Illness*, Norman Cousins states that, "What happens in the body can affect the brain, and what happens in the brain can affect the body. Hope, purpose and determination are not merely mental states. They have electrochemical connections that play a large part in the workings of the immune systems."

A related phenomenon is laughter. Results of a study at the UCLA Johnson Cancer Center show that after patients laugh, their pain thresholds double, which can potentially help patients with disorders such as arthritis, or patients who require chemotherapy, dialysis or burn treatments. If you thought it was hard to feel happy in a slouched position, try laughing with your chin in your chest. Your body won't speak that language!

I believe that this brain-body relationship affects the medical outcome for many ill people. If you can think and act positively, despite your cancer diagnosis, you will be happier and less stressed. It's natural to be distressed with a cancer diagnosis, and not everyone has a naturally optimistic personality. People who don't have to work at it.

Besides optimism, another important quality is your willingness to be an active participant in your own treatment. Being active can improve the outcome by making you determined to get the best possible treatment, or to maximize the effectiveness of the treatment you receive. When diagnosed with an illness, you can either lose hope or decide to take a new lease on life. With today's detailed prognoses, you could feel sufficiently devastated to become self-destructive. But with a purpose, a goal and inspiration, you can decide to control your own destiny.

My friend, Cindy, was diagnosed with breast cancer in 2005. Before and after surgery, you could not tell anything was wrong. I watched in awe as she brought her kids to and from practices and activities. She held her head high. To this day, many people assume that Cindy experienced neither pain nor disappointments. She jokes often about her "new boobs." That's Attitude with a capitol A. Cindy had an attitude of believing that bolstered her self-image and helped to create the outcome she needed.

Dressing for Attitude

Another important aspect of body language is attire. How you dress affects both how you feel and how you act, as does grooming in general. If you are trying to develop a more confident, positive attitude, try to choose clothing that matches that goal. I don't know about you, but I've seen enough flip-flops and t-shirts to last me a lifetime. The sight of super-casual-bordering-on-sloppy attire does nothing to build confidence in me, and I can't believe it does much for the wearer either. You don't have to spend a lot of money to be attractively and appropriately dressed. Nor do you have to be uncomfortable. However, you might need to give your wardrobe a little more attention than you are giving it now.

One of the most popular recurring themes on the *Oprah* TV show is the makeover. Audiences love the remarkable transformations achieved by simply changing a person's hair style and clothing. Part of the appeal is that more than mere appearance is usually affected. The person moves and talks differently, and the glow of transformation seems to come from inside.

My son once had a tennis coach whom the parents ridiculed. Yes, me included. We didn't make fun of her personally. What provoked our mirth was her style of coaching. She carried index cards with all aspects of the game written on them. Yet she had one simple remedy for every possible mistake a player could make: *Stop it!*

Double faulting? The solution was, *Stop it!* Missing overheads? The remedy was, *Stop it!* It was a hoot.

Ironically, I now realize that she was 100 percent right. Not only that, I have incorporated that tennis instructor's style in my program of attitude control.

Feeling down? *Stop it!*

Feel like quitting? *Stop it!*

Feel ugly? *Stop it!*

Feel frustrated? *Stop it!*

Feel good about yourself. Teach yourself to rebound. Square your shoulders and go to war against negative self-talk. People who feel good about themselves produce good results. People who feel lousy about themselves produce negative results. Believe me, it's true. Hold your head high, pretend to have everything under control and soon you will. Energy—positive, mind-altering energy. Wear it and wear it well.

Exercise #9
Body Language in Prime Time

Objectives

The purpose of this exercise is to develop awareness of the importance of body language and to test your ability to interpret the nonverbal behaviors of others, including facial expressions, gestures, posture and gait.

Materials

Television, DVD player and movie; paper and pencil

Time required

At least 30 minutes, more if desired

Procedure

1. Rent or borrow a movie with considerable dramatic content. Choose one that you have not seen before and don't know very much about.

2. Watch at least 30 minutes of the movie *with the sound turned off.* Pay close attention to the body language of the characters (facial expressions, gestures, posture, movements). Write down the emotions that the characters are portraying. Keep a running list and make notes to indicate what evidence led to your conclusion. For example, if you decide that a character feels terrified, indicate that terror shows in her wide eyes, open mouth, furrowed brow, shrinking posture, etc.

3. Replay the same segment *with the sound turned on.* Check your conclusions against the dialogue. How often did you read the body language of the characters correctly? What emotions did you have trouble identifying?

4. For at least one full day, pay close attention to the body language of *every* person with whom you come in contact. Concentrate on improving your ability to accurately "read" body language. And don't forget to apply what you learn to your own body language.

Variations

Instead of watching 30 straight minutes at the beginning of the film, use the DVD scene selector to skip from one part of the movie to another. Watch 5 to 10 minutes from each scene. Do this exercise with one or more other people and compare interpretations. Have a friendly competition to see who is the most skillful interpreter of body language.

STOP

Think about what you have learned from this chapter. Review your reactions and decide how you will use this information.

10

Practicing Positive Self-Talk

I ran into old friends Bob and Libby at the airport a couple of years ago and observed that Bob's head looked severely burned. I quickly asked what was going on and learned that he had been diagnosed with cancer during a routine dermatological exam.

Bob had a beautiful smile on his face and a calmness about him. After talking a few minutes, I was convinced that his attitude was genuine—not merely an attempt to make me feel comfortable. Furthermore, he was more interested in learning about me and my family than in talking about his illness. He impressed me as a beautiful person with a beautiful spirit.

Later, I asked Libby how Bob felt when he was given the news. She described a man with abundant tenacity, energy, humor and the will to live. Right from the start, he wanted to get to work and focus on the next treatment step. He was too busy living to waste undue time being sick. His attitude has remained optimistic and upbeat throughout treatment.

Of course, when one person in the family is sick, everybody is affected. Bob and Libby are such great partners that when she is down he lifts her up, and when he's down she encourages him. They have walked hand-in-hand through the entire remarkable journey.

Bob's attitude is, "I don't have time to get sick. Let's get on with this, I have golf to play." However, the couple does admit being angry in the beginning. Referring to the first two of the classic five stages of grief theorized by Elisabeth Kubler Ross, Libby laughed and explained, "We skipped denial and went straight to anger." A sense of humor is so important.

Many of us go through life in a perpetual pity-party because we're mad at our husband, mad at the children, mad that we don't have a career, mad that we can't seem to stick to an exercise program. The negative input we funnel through our heads all the time limits us from doing more, achieving more, and following through on our goals and plans to *be* more.

A Steady Commentary

You talk to yourself constantly, often without realizing you are doing so. Your brain produces a running thought commentary on everything you feel, think and do, like the breaking news reports that run across the bottom of the TV screen. This "self-talk" can range from uplifting to depressing, and your demeanor often reflects where on the scale it falls. If the words are positive and encouraging, your body language and attitude are upbeat. If the words are harsh and critical, your body language and attitude are dull and pessimistic. A lot of subliminal self-talk is stored up during life's journey that can slow down or stall our progress. We must constantly strive to replace that voice with new and good information. So talk sweetly to yourself—and with respect.

If you have the habit of engaging in critical self-talk, changing the nature of the chatter won't be easy. First, become aware of your thoughts—pay attention to how your mind reacts to experiences of all kinds and, in particular, mistakes (yours or those of other people). Lift each thought out of the background noise and examine it for accuracy and usefulness. Most of the time, negative self-talk is made up of gross simplifications and exaggerations. When you burn your finger and say to yourself, "You stupid idiot," you are being both dishonest and lazy. First, you are neither stupid nor an idiot. Second, you just missed a chance to assess the real reason for the mishap and learn some useful information. You took the easy way out and called yourself a name. (You may have the same tendency when responding to other people in conflict situations, resorting to name calling and easy labels instead of actually listening to what they have to say. It's a sorry habit, and distressingly common.)

Once you become aware of your self-talk, stop yourself when you "hear" something negative and immediately replace it with an accurate, neutral-to-positive thought. For example, replace, "You stupid idiot," with "Oops. I wasn't paying attention. I'd better get my mind on what I'm doing." That's neutral and accurate. Suppose you submit some important market projections at the office and later find out they contained serious miscalculations. You think, "Well, there goes my promotion. The boss won't want a dunce like me in the corner office." Stop yourself and think instead, "This is a good lesson. I'll figure out what went wrong, so it won't happen again." That is a positive and helpful thought. Thomas Edison failed thousands of times before he successfully developed the incandescent light bulb. When he was asked how he felt about all those failures, he replied, "I have not failed. I've just found 10,000 ways that won't work." If he hadn't maintained a positive attitude, you might be reading this book by candlelight.

When I work with a large group, I sometimes ask, "How many of you were raised by parents who talked about the importance of a positive attitude?" Very few people respond affirmatively. When I ask, "Do you usually talk to yourself in a supportive way, or a negative way?" many folks don't really understand what I'm getting at. So I explain, "A 60-word-per-minute typist sounds like this (and I pound on the table). In contrast, this is how fast you talk to yourself—over 100 words per minute (and I frantically slam on the table)."

You think a fast typist is exceptional. You hear the clicking and think you should pour water on the computer keys. But, honestly, you talk to yourself much more rapidly than a typist can type—over 1,000 words per minute. What are you saying?

Are you criticizing yourself and putting yourself down. Or is your self-talk positive and helpful?

To be successful, you must be enthusiastic about your daily routines and build success by establishing and accomplishing goals. Don't let negative experiences determine your self-esteem. We all have them—they are as much a part of life as the air we breathe. When a relationship sours, figure out what went wrong so that you won't repeat the same mistakes the next time around. If you fail to achieve a goal, evaluate the outcome. Maybe the goal was unrealistic to begin with, or you were lacking critical information, or simply didn't work hard enough. Then, instead of saying to yourself, "I failed," say "I learned a valuable lesson and I'll do better next time." Toot your own horn! If future performances are improved by the knowledge, you are justified in counting it as a net gain.

Make it a goal to employ this "flip-side technique" throughout the day, every day. Turn each negative around and make it a positive. Instead of saying, "I have to go to work," say "I *get* to go to work." Instead of dreading an out-of-town business trip, think, "This trip will give me a change of scenery and a new experience." Replace "I can't believe how much we have to do—we'll never make it," with, "Maybe we can finish up tomorrow and still be on target, but with less stress. I *know* we can do it."

If your self-talk improves a small amount weekly, you will soon begin to see, feel and expect great things. Like the little blue choo-choo train, thinking and believing you *can* will see you through the steepest climb.

Strong Leads

The leading words of a sentence often set the tone for what follows. Strong, unequivocal beginnings are best. For example, instead of saying "I'll try," say "I will." Replace "I don't know" with "I'll find out." Memorize these "leads" and use them to make your self-talk more positive:

I can …
I must …
I will …
I know there is hope because …

I have the opportunity to …
I like myself because …
I am motivated about …
I feel encouraged by …
I love …
I am good at …

Accentuate the Positive

People who feel good about themselves produce good results, which is why you should make a consistent effort to have favorable thoughts about yourself. Make a list of your positive traits. Briefly describe specific examples that prove you have these qualities. If your list includes "loyal," write down three or four recent instances of loyal behavior. If it includes "artistic," describe two or three artistic accomplishments. Your examples don't have to be worthy of medals and blue ribbons. They can be very small things that no one else knows about. For example, maybe you have a talent for seeing the "big picture," facilitating social interaction, or mediating disagreements. The idea is to think about these abilities and focus on them, to allow them to become part of your self-talk. The payoff is improved self-esteem.

Many of us focus on our faults and weaknesses and practically ignore our strengths. We spend time and money trying to "fix" ourselves and feeling inadequate if we don't succeed. I frequently see this in organizations. A company hires or promotes a person to fill a position for which he or she is ill-suited and then tries to mold the person to fit the job. A better approach would be to choose someone with the appropriate talents and skills to begin with. Sounds obvious, doesn't it? But you'd be surprised how often companies shortcut the hiring process and pay for it later. We do the same thing to ourselves. We pay for our negative focus in endless personal dissatisfaction. I'm not suggesting that you ignore your weaknesses and make no effort to improve yourself, just that you spend an equal or greater amount of time developing your strengths and talents and putting them to good use.

Facilitating Focus

Life is full of opportunities to use self-talk to strengthen focus. Focus is extremely important when you are pursuing a goal of any kind. Think of the aerialist crossing a tightrope. He must focus intently on where he is going, knowing and visualizing the outcome while giving full attention to each step and the delicate adjustments necessary to maintain balance on the way to his goal.

My dad had a remedy for carsickness that involved focus. He would tell me to carefully cut a quarter-sized circle out of a brown paper bag. If it wasn't perfect, he'd make me do it again. After I had the perfect coin-shaped circle, I held the piece of paper in the center of my neck. The circle had to be positioned in just the right spot. The psychology of my dad's remedy was simple. While I concentrated my attention on cutting out the circle and holding it against my neck, my focus was drawn away from thoughts of illness.

I use this same principle when teaching my children about God and their relationship with Him. In *My Utmost for His Highest*, Oswald Chambers and James Reimann urge Christians: "Never allow anything to deflect you from insight into Jesus Christ. Don't move your eyes from the Cross—look only toward your heavenly goal. Keep your eyes upon Jesus and the Cross." I employ this same method at church. A long time ago, I learned to sit up front where I cannot see all of the other people. If I can see them, my mind wanders and I think about them instead of the message of the service. Sitting up front helps me focus.

Almost 18 years ago, during the early stages of my sickness, a friend passed along to me a copy of Agnes Sanford's book, *The Healing Light*. More than a dozen years later, at a low point in my recovery, I searched for the book on every shelf of my library as though ransacking the refrigerator for food.

Sanford's writing is a great source of strength. She illustrates that God is both *within* us and *without* us. She writes, "He is the source of all life; the creator of the universe behind universe; and unimaginable depths of inter-stellar space and of light-years without end. But He is also the indwelling life of our own little selves. And just as a whole world full of electricity will not light a house unless the house itself is prepared to receive that electricity, so the infinite and eternal life of God cannot help us unless we are prepared to receive that life within ourselves."

Sanford describes four prayer steps. First, she says, we must contact God, by relaxing and realizing that there is a source of life outside ourselves. Second, we must connect with God through prayer. Third, we must believe that God's power is flowing into us. No matter how much we ask for something, it becomes our own only when we accept it and give thanks for it. Fourth, we must accomplish something tangible in order to determine if our experience succeeded or failed.

Many people are afraid to take the fourth step. They are afraid they will fail and lose faith. Others live with the illusion that prayers are granted like wishes, with no effort on the part of the petitioner. But prayer requires both focus and action. Case in point: my 15-year-old son, Ryan.

Ryan has always been a busy child, participating in sports and school events. He goes nonstop throughout the day and wears himself out, so he generally goes to bed earlier than the rest of us. However, awhile back I noticed that Ryan was staying up later, pacing the floor above my bedroom and keeping me awake.

When I mentioned the change to Ryan and asked him to please be courteous of other family members, he casually nodded and apologized. However, a few days later he came to me and asked if I ever had trouble maintaining my thoughts, especially during prayer. Ryan shared with me that he could no longer focus during his bedtime prayers. So instead of praying quietly, he paced his room while talking to God aloud. This enabled him to maintain his concentration. I felt horrible knowing that my complaints had interrupted his conversations with God.

Often, success or failure will depend on our ability to focus. It is that tiny effort of attention that allows us to think clearly concerning our choices. So ask yourself, do you want to schedule an appointment with God, or opt for watching TV or doing the laundry?

Self-talk and Healing

I frequently coach people who have serious, often life-threatening, diseases. One of the things we work very hard on is self-talk.

You can be diagnosed with cancer today and look at it as an opportunity to change your existence—to think differently and to turn your attention to the finer things in life. You can say to yourself that you are glad it is one type of cancer instead of another, because your chances for recovery are better. You can think to yourself, "I'm going to lick this thing and keep going. This is the first day of the rest of my life. I am going to be an active participant in the treatment and I am going to become a better person." This is positive thinking—prosperity thinking! Another person diagnosed with the same type of cancer on the same day might walk away thinking that death is imminent, go home and crawl into bed. That person has concluded that life today is drastically different than it was yesterday, and *it is not*.

Months or years down the road the differences between these two reactions will continue to play out. The person who thinks positively will accomplish more, become emotionally and spiritually stronger, and may live longer, too.

I used to frequent the same gym as Greg, who had Stage 4 stomach cancer. He would visit the gym after his chemotherapy treatments and run on the treadmill, chanting to himself while rubbing his stomach. Over and over again, he would repeat, "Attack these nasty cancer cells in my body. Strengthen me. Heal me." This type of self-talk feeds powerful imagery to the subconscious mind.

In *The Magic of Believing*, author Claude Bristol compares subconscious suggestion to a seedling in nature: "…Plant the right kind of seed-thought of a pure strain, and habitually feed it with strong affirmative thought always directed toward the same end, and it will grow into a mighty force, finding ways of overcoming all obstacles. It will reach forth with its roots to find more food on which to grow and expand its foliage to gather more sunshine."

In today's world, doctors and scientists understand that the mind and the body are fundamentally related. Simply put, what happens in your body will affect your subconscious and what happens in your subconscious will affect your body. It is hard for doctors to determine what percentage of an illness is physical and what percentage is mental. For instance, migraine sufferers experience real pain, but they are also anxious and distressed over the pain.

If you can convince yourself that a challenger is soft, your subconscious will accept the challenger as inferior to you and act accordingly. Visualizing the challenger, whether person or disease, as an irrelevant opponent transforms the situation into something you can reasonably undertake.

In *The Magic of Believing*, Claude M. Bristol writes of a young lawyer who was terrified the first time he faced a brilliant opposing counsel. To fortify his courage, the lawyer thought to himself, "I'm just as good as he is; as a matter of fact, I'm better. I can lick him and I will." With his eyes closed, he repeated the phrase over and over and, after several seconds, felt like he could tackle the challenge. He continued to practice the ritual before difficult cases and unenthusiastic juries.

Think of your illness as opposing counsel in a trial over the fate of your life. Close your eyes and repeat, "I am stronger than this disease. I can beat it and will." Argue your case convincingly and relentlessly.

In his book *Peace, Love & Healing*, Bernie S. Siegel writes of a man with a terminal illness whose friend sent him to one of Siegel's workshops. Siegel, who specializes in self-healing, self-love and determination, gave the man a chance to be heroic. The man accepted the challenge. Siegel has the ability to inspire hope and, through that hope, facilitates the healing of lives. Writes Siegel, "(The terminally-ill man) decided not to give up, and he felt good about his decision. To me that's miracle enough—especially now that we're beginning to discover something about the physiological consequences of optimism. ...I believe in using hope to facilitate change in the healing of lives."

If you are ill, look forward to a positive resolution. Don't take your eyes or attitude off of a joyful outcome. Visualize your body being 100 percent healthy. Speak positive affirmations to yourself during times of turmoil. Tell yourself that you deserve a sound body, completely free of disease.

In *The New Medicine*, a companion book to the public television series by the same name, authors Ronald H. Blumer and Muffie Meyer interview Dr. Ester M. Sternberg, a research professor at American University about the relationship of mental state to sickness and health.

Sternberg notes that for thousands of years people believed that, "Stress could make you sick, that believing could make you well, and that your social world affects your health."

While mothers passed down this interpretation to their children for centuries, Sternberg says that the scientific and medical community did not believe these concepts. Up until 20 years ago, the notion that the brain and the immune system communicate— that the immune system sends signals to the brain and in turn, the brain regulates how the immune system functions—was revolutionary. Sternberg's colleagues criticized researchers who were working in the field. She was told that studying the effects of emotions on healing would ruin her career.

Through the advances of cellular and molecular biology in the mid-20th century, Sternberg says physicians and scientists now understand how the immune system works. She states, "Now, with the brain imaging of molecular biology, cell biology, and physiology, we can put all the pieces of the puzzle together, which we certainly could not do even a few decades ago. So the good news is that those very technologies that once obscured the thoughtful, caring side of medicine now can be used to understand how emotions and health are one."

Exercise #10

Improving Your Self-Talk

Objectives

The purpose of this exercise is to generate positive thoughts and statements about yourself. Most of us engage in a great deal of negative self-talk—scolding ourselves for mistakes and perceived weaknesses. The objective here is to do the opposite.

Materials

Writing materials or computer

Time required

About 20 minutes

Procedure

1. Finish the following sentences:

   I feel successful in my present job because…
   Two examples of how I look for the positive in others are…
   I am comfortable in new situations because…
   I appreciate receiving criticism because…
   I am optimistic about…
   A goal I recently achieved is…
   Others respect me because…
   A valuable lesson I learned from a recent mistake is…
   I like who I am because…

2. Look over the sentences that you have written. Select three or four that are highly affirmative and use them as affirmations. An affirmation is a positive statement that you repeat to yourself with conviction and feeling. An example from the above list is, "I am comfortable in new situations." If repeated regularly, this affirmation should help you approach new situations with greater calm and confidence.

STOP

Think about what you have learned from this chapter. Review your reactions and decide how you will use this information.

11

Mailboxing

My older sister and I had our differences growing up. She seemed to enjoy chipping away at my self-esteem. Granted, most siblings fight and many experience bouts of mutual jealousy. However, I always had the feeling that Jackie was judging me. She was extremely critical, and I always knew just what she was thinking. The irony is, she was right when she told me that I was different, that I danced to the beat of a different drummer. She'd roll her eyes and speculate that I must be adopted. Oftentimes I hoped I was.

My sister was correct—I did dance to a different beat, and I'm glad. I'm also happy that she mentioned adoption. If she hadn't planted that seed years ago, my husband and I might have stopped after having three children of our own. Instead we adopted three more beautiful children, one from Russia and two from Guatemala. Talk about people dancing to the beat of different drummers—all six of our kids do.

I invented *Mailboxing*® many years ago when I headed out the door to work one morning leaving a toddler with strep behind in the care of a babysitter. Chronically stressed from an ugly divorce, I sat beside my mailbox and cried my eyes out. After several minutes I thought, "You know, I am going to put Matthew in this mailbox." Obviously I didn't mean physically, I meant emotionally. I stood up, pulled down the mailbox door and proclaimed aloud, "There goes Matthew."

Now, I know and you know and the world knows that Matthew's mother was the best person to give him the antibiotic prescribed by his pediatrician. But on that day it just wasn't going to happen. I was going to put him in the mailbox, and the babysitter would have the right to give him the medicine, and I would have the right not to worry.

Then I started thinking about how hard it was to own my home and be divorced and in business, with bank loans and all the other things that weighed on my mind at night when I was exhausted. I told myself, "It's hard to carry the divorce to work every day. In fact, it's painful and humiliating to discuss both the infidelity and the divorce. I will not go to work and waste my energy talking about it. I am going to take a vacation from it."

And, just like that, I stuck the divorce in the mailbox.

On the way to work I focused on just what I could accomplish that day with the time I had. When I arrived at work, I picked up the phone and called my babysitter. I told her that from that day forward I would not be calling three times a day to check on Matt. In fact, I would not be calling *at all*, and if my staff told me the babysitter was on the phone, I would know to head straight for the car and rush home, because it was an emergency. I explained that I had to be able to focus on work while at work and on home while at home. I was going to separate the two so completely that I would be a different person at each place.

I telephoned family members—people who often called to schedule lunch dates or just chat—and told them the same thing. I decided to make my business the very best temporary service in existence. I got married to my career that day and vowed to stop jumping back and forth between professional and personal issues. I named this process *Mailboxing*®.

That evening when I arrived home, I opened the mailbox and took out Matthew and the antibiotic and the strep throat. I took out the babysitter, the divorce and the bills. They didn't look as bad as they had when I put them in there. In fact, they looked a great deal more manageable.

I still mailbox more than 20 years later. I know in my mind and heart that we deserve breaks from different parts of our lives. When we take breaks, our shoulders don't feel so burdened and weighted down, and we deal more effectively with people. It's like taking a mini-vacation. When you go on vacation you come back refreshed, often with a lot of new ideas. Things look better than they did when you left.

I made other deposits in the mailbox. Some evenings it was the banker with whom I had trouble getting an increased line of credit because I was young and female. I looked like an adolescent driving a 1963 Volkswagen with rusted out floorboards, and the bank didn't think much of my collateral. The mailbox also got all of my unsatisfied clients and a slew of petty office arguments, employee reprimands and sad luck stories. I stopped at the mailbox twice a day, every day—going and coming.

Narrowing Your Focus

One of the things we tend to do, if we're not careful, is short-change the people we love. We don't hug or kiss them. In our preoccupation, we don't give them very much of anything. Mentally and emotionally we are already at the office when we should be focusing on the family. Without positive attention, relationships deteriorate and become dysfunctional.

Mailboxing® not only helps us improve relationships with our loved ones at home, it also allows our careers to flourish. By focusing on the task at hand, we are able to produce a better product.

During the Depression era of the 1930s, a group of grocery store managers came to self-help consultant Claude M. Bristol for help. Noted for his philosophy that the energy of the subconscious mind can help individuals achieve any goal, Bristol persuaded the managers to use his science to push the sale of specific items one day a week.

"The day before each sale, the managers carefully coached their clerks to make a mental picture of each customer coming into their stores and buying the selected items," he writes in *The Magic of Believing.*

The effect of the visualization was astonishing. The store that specialized in cheese sold more cheese in that one day it had in the previous six months. The shop that featured beef rolled roast and the one that featured fresh salmon sold more on their respective feature days than all the others stores combined. The store where squash was the featured item had to call for replenishments twice during the day.

By focusing on the sales of one particular item, the store managers were able to accomplish their goals. They weren't visualizing bills that had to be paid, or other tasks that had to be done. Their main focus during the day was to sell the featured item. At the end of the day, after selling out of the particular product, that managers were probably able to go home and spend more quality time with family because they accomplished their objectives.

Mailboxing® is hard to do at first. However, once you get the hang of it, you will be happier, your family will be happier and all the people at work will be happier. When you shortchange your family, you are telling them that work is more important than they are. And I don't care how you say it. I don't care if you get on your high horse and proclaim, "Well, if I didn't work we wouldn't have a house and vacations and nice things." I don't care what you say. What it boils down to is that work is more important to you than they are. I don't know of one person who, on their death bed, said, "I wish I had spent more time at the office."

Conserving Energy

Mailboxing® is a form of compartmentalization. When you compartmentalize your responsibilities, you mentally wall them off from one another so that you can focus on one at a time. When you compartmentalize your worries, you mentally separate them from one another so that you don't become overwhelmed with stress.

President Bill Clinton was famous for his ability compartmentalize. He did not allow the stress of impeachment, or any other specific issue he was dealing with, to interfere with other responsibilities. People were in awe of his upbeat attitude. Some thought he was insensitive and callous to the embarrassment of the nation during the impeachment. They thought he should appear shamefaced and remorseful. What he was actually doing was tantamount to *Mailboxing*®.

A woman whose child collapsed on the playing field and, but for a handy defibrillator, would have died of cardiac arrest, was so overcome with the grief and horror of having almost lost her son that she could barely function, even after the episode was over. One day, to avoid continuously re-experiencing the pain of those terrible hours, she closed her eyes and envisioned a small, empty room with an open door. She took all of her pain and anguish, pushed it into the room and closed the door. Then she nailed the door shut, concealed it with drywall and several coats of paint, making it disappear. That powerful visualization freed her of the emotional pain so that she could once again function normally. It, too, was a form of *Mailboxing*®.

Mailboxing® conserves energy. Trying to devote energy to numerous problems at the same time can quickly lead to physical and emotional exhaustion. Even when you think you are focusing on only one problem, others are often lurking in the background causing tense shoulders, knots in the stomach and a general feeling of worry or dread. No single problem, no matter how important, receives your undivided attention when you are in a state of perpetual distraction. The vivid imagery created by mentally or symbolically putting issues in the mailbox, knowing that you will remove and deal with them at a later, more appropriate time, has been extremely effective for most of the people to whom I have taught this process.

Mailboxing® has a calming influence because it puts you in greater control of your life. When I arrived at work after having put Mathew, the babysitter, the medicine, and dozens of other personal and domestic matters into the mailbox, I felt relaxed and focused. I no longer worried about having to be all things to all people, all at the same time. When I arrived home, I would not enter the house until I had made the exchange, trading my business life for my personal life. It was a joy to have finally found a way to keep them separate.

Exercise #11

Into the Mailbox

Objectives:

- To avoid carrying around problems all day that can't be resolved at work.

- To avoid carrying around problems all evening/weekend that can't be resolved at home.

Materials:

- Two makeshift mailboxes—boxes with removable lids and a slot in the top, decorated to suit your fancy. (Remember those boxes you designed in elementary school for Valentine's Day?)

- small note pads and pencils (two each)

Time required:

5 minutes, twice a day—before leaving for work, and before leaving work for home

Procedure:

1. Construct the mailboxes. Place one next to the front door at home. Place the other on your desk at work, or next to the door through which you exit.

2. In the morning before walking out the door, quickly jot down any worries, resentments, frustrations, or plans related to home and family that threaten to plague you throughout the workday. Fold up the piece of paper. Put a date on it and drop it in the mailbox. As you do so, say to yourself, "These things will be waiting for me when I get home. I will *not* think about them at work."

3. In the evening before leaving work, quickly jot down any personnel problems, office politics, unfinished assignments, and other concerns that threaten to bug you all night. Fold up the paper, date it and drop it in the box on your desk while saying, "These things will be waiting for me when I arrive at work tomorrow. I will *not* think about them at home."

4. When you get home, remove the lid from the home mailbox and take out that morning's list. Open it up and read through the list. Some of the items probably won't matter to you anymore. Great. Decide what to do about the rest of the items. Congratulate yourself on not letting home issues interfere with your workday.

5. When you arrive at work the next day, remove the lid from the office mailbox and take out the previous evening's list. Again, some of the items will no longer seem important. Forget them. Decide what to do about the rest. Congratulate yourself on successfully leaving work issues at the office.

6. Stop at each mailbox twice a day. Drop off a list when you leave. Pick up the same list when you return.

Note: You are probably thinking that you can't always leave home issues at home and work issues at work. My response is, nobody can *always* do anything, but if you are trying to make your life better, more reasonable and happier, you must take the right steps with the correct attitude. Modify the exercise if you like. Do your best to make it work for you.

STOP

Think about what you have learned from this chapter. Review your reactions and decide how you will use this information.

Postscript

In closing, I want to remind you that attitude is an assertive behavior—for better or worse, attitude affects everything you do. It should belong to the part of you that wants to do more, the part that wants to do better. I don't know about you, but I want to achieve. I want to know that if I'm dealt a problem I can handle it. I can confront it head-on and not back down, and not be afraid. I want to get the problem in a headlock and come up the winner.

Employers used to measure workers by their experience, degrees and professional accomplishments. In the 21st century they will measure employees by attitude as well, and by how they respond to criticism and stress. They will look very favorably on employees who understand how their attitude affects the job performance of themselves and their coworkers, and the growth of the company.

Several years ago I sold a business that had thousands of employees. Looking back, the ones who stand out in my mind are the ones who, no matter what you threw at them, no matter what came their way, no matter what a customer did, made life easier on those around them.

Many of the cancer patients I work with want to defeat their illness. And if they can't, they want to at least go down feeling a sense of strength and pride for having tried their best and taken good care of themselves in the process.

Everyone wants to get better, but many of us don't know how. When we face overwhelming circumstances, it's hard to see the forest for the trees. Say to yourself daily, "Just for today, I will try..." and fill in the ending with one or more of the lessons you have learned from reading this book.

We live among modern miracles. We need to open our eyes and minds to see them and feel their impact. We need to look for miracles in our own lives, and we need to make them happen. Don't just sit back and wait, become proactive, allowing miracles to happen. When miracles occur, talk about their spiritual meaning. Such stories are uplifting. They help others who are hurting to tear down the emotional barriers that prevent their having positive thoughts.

Where you stand is not as important as the direction in which you are moving. Keep moving in the right direction.

References

Heart, Bear and Larkin, Molly, *The Wind Is My Mother*. New York: Clarkson Potter Publishers, 1996.

Black, Claudia, *It's Never Too Late to Have a Happy Childhood*. New York: Ballantine Books, 1989.

Blumer, Ronald H. and Meyer, Muffie, *The New Medicine*. New York: Middlemarch Films, 2006.

Bristol, Claude M., *The Magic of Believing*. New York: Prentice Hall, 1948.

Buscaglia, Leo F., *Personhood*. New York: Fawcett Columbine, 1978.

Cousins, Norman, *Anatomy of an Illness as Perceived by the Patient*. Bantam, 1991.

Girard, Vickmie, *There's No Place Like Hope*. Lynnwood, WA: Compendium, Inc., 2001.

Ryan, M.J., *The Power of Patience*. New York: Broadway Books, 2003.

Sanford, Agnes, *The Healing Light*. New York: Ballantine Books, 1947.

Siegel, Bernie S., *Peace, Love and Healing*. New York: Harper & Row, Publishers, 1989.

Whitfield, Charles L., *Healing the Child Within*. Deerfield Beach, FL: Health Communications, 1988.

REFERENCES

21 Stories

Have you ever walked down the corridor of a hospital, glancing into some of the rooms, and realized just how lucky you are? When I was a child, a popular precept that was passed on to me was to "walk a mile in another man's shoes." How would it feel to be in the shoes of one of those patients in the hospital?

I have included these 21 brief stories to encourage you to develop empathy, change your attitude and attain your goals in life. It takes 21 days to form a habit. Please read one story a day for the next 21 days until the habit of feeling grateful for your life has become ingrained. If your life is more miserable and tragic than the lives of the people in these stories, find comfort in the knowledge that others who suffer have learned to maintain a positive outlook. Learn from them.

1

Aaron

Aaron is proud to call West Virginia his home. As a youngster, fun was a priority, but with his competitive edge, he also liked to win. Aaron grew up in a very traditional home. His father went to work while his mother's job was at home. He lived a perfect life. However, something led Aaron to experiment with drugs and alcohol while he was in junior high and he continued on that path until his mid-thirties. He recalls a blur of treatment centers and jail, and describes reaching his lowest low at his 36th birthday celebration. His mother asked Aaron to refrain from alcohol for the family dinner, but the evening was a disaster. Aaron wonders just what she expected. He was using cocaine and drinking up to one-half gallon of bourbon a day. At times he would go through thousands of dollars worth of cocaine. People occasionally found him unconscious.

Perhaps the pivotal moment occurred when Aaron faced death. He was at the lower depths of rock bottom. On his apartment floor, he prayed to God. He said he felt a warmth in his body and knew he was healed. God forgave him and also took away all the addictions. He stopped taking drugs, ingesting alcohol, smoking cigarettes, and following a lifestyle that would probably have killed him.

Aaron was called to the ministry about 12 years ago and all his unhealthy cravings have ceased. He is certain that this miracle was delivered by God and feels privileged and blessed to be able to share his story so that others will be more inclined to harbor an attitude of forgiveness toward their own circumstances. Aaron's advice is to never give up. Separate yourself from past environments and friends in order to divorce your addictions. No matter how many attempts you have made, a healthy life is worth another try. You will get there. You must believe in yourself and speak as encouragingly to yourself as you would to your best friend.

2

Ditty

Sometimes it seems that things happen for a reason. Ditty is a licensed professional counselor. In the fall of 2002, while obtaining the necessary credits to maintain her licensure, Ditty studied hypnosis at West Virginia University. She was intrigued by the subject and sometimes practiced the technique on her husband, Gary.

About a year later, Gary fell off a ladder at their home, hitting his head. On arrival at the hospital, Gary became very combative, and nothing the staff tried succeeded in quieting him. Ditty asked if she could try hypnosis. Skeptically, the hospital acquiesced. Her treatment appeared to work and Gary grew calm.

Gary's condition was like a roller coaster. He would appear to get better and then worsen. About a month after the fall, he suffered a seizure from an undiagnosed aneurism and went into a coma. He was placed in intensive care and his condition was grave.

The tragedy brought Gary's family together. The couple's youngest son, Penn, in his junior year of college, moved home to be with his father. Now, after returning to school and graduating, he has taken a job close by. Peter, their oldest son, was a practicing attorney in Charleston. He too stayed close to home until his dad was back on his feet.

Ditty, in addition to providing her husband with much loving support, has assumed the role of taskmaster. She encourages, or, rather, pushes Gary to persist in his recovery. Their relationship was always great, but they now have a true and kindred appreciation for each other.

Ditty called upon the writings of Dr. Ron Havens, author of *Hypnotherapy Scripts*, who strongly supports the theory that the brain hears and responds to indirect suggestions. The book is replete with inductions, which are verses used to bring subjects in and out of trances. Ditty chose one entitled, "Wakeful Awareness." After she repeated the verse several times, Gary came out of the coma.

Ditty does not deprecate the work of Gary's neurosurgeon and the team of skilled medical professionals that she credits with Gary's ultimate recovery. However, she and Gary believe that hypnosis played a role. Hypnosis has become another tool in her counseling toolbox. She believes that faith will pull people through traumas and that they must not sit around feeling sorry for themselves and their situations.

3

Rick and Kim

Rick and Kim are an awesome couple. They are the parents of exceptional sons who serve God and have blessed Rick and Kim with superior grandchildren.

In June of 2004 they received a telephone call that toppled their world. David, their son, had been killed in a fiery crash in Florida. A tractor trailer had hit David and his missionary companions head on and burned them beyond recognition. How do parents take the news that their child is dead and, because of the nature of the accident, no physical trace of him remains? How do they cope? How do they get up the next day and put one foot in front of the other?

Rick and Kim told me that they needed a lot of comfort and consolation. They said they, "ran to the medicine cabinet of God's word and found the prescription they needed." That prescription was scripture. Psalm 13: 1-5 contains this plea for God's help: "How long must I be hiding daily anguish in my heart? How long shall my enemy have the upper hand? Answer me, O Lord my God; give me light in my darkness lest I die."

I have witnessed the strength and resolve of this family. People who love them agree that they have shown amazing courage.

Rick and Kim asked to conclude their story with the following additional words of scripture:

"Let not your heart be troubled: ye believe in God, believe also in me. In my Father's house are many mansions: if it were not so, I would have told you. I go to prepare a place for you. And if I go and prepare a place for you, I will come again, and receive you unto myself; that where I am, There ye may be also. And whither I

go ye know, and the way ye know. Thomas saith unto him, Lord, we know not whither thou goest; and how can we know the way? Jesus saith unto him, I am the way, the truth, and the life: no man cometh unto the Father, but by me." (John 14: 1-6)

4

Becky

Becky's mother deserted her when she was two years old. Her father was, in her words, a "wild child," so she, her brother and sister were reared by their paternal grandparents.

Becky was led to believe that her mother was no longer in the vicinity, so imagine her surprise when at age 15 she learned from a cousin that her mother had always lived on the other side of town with another brother, sister, and a stepbrother Becky knew nothing about.

Becky paid a brief visit to her mother, but the reunion was awkward, so they had very little contact until Becky was 25. At that point, they began seeing each other once or twice a year at picnics and other events, and occasionally talked on the phone. Becky's mother explained that she had given up custody because she thought the grandparents could give Becky a better life than she could. Becky believed in her heart that this was true.

In 2005, Becky received a call from her brother telling her that their mother was in the hospital and was not doing well. Becky started spending more time with her mother, running errands, picking up prescriptions and going with her mother to medical appointments. In the six months before her mother's death in

2006, the two became very close. They expressed their love for one another for the first time just months before Becky's mother died.

According to Becky, if one positive thing came from her mother's death, it was the opportunity to know her younger siblings and experience a sense of family. She and her brothers and sisters went through the tragedy of their mother's death together, holding and depending upon one another, and crying on one another's shoulders.

Throughout this entire experience, Becky has maintained an attitude of forgiveness, feeling in her heart that her mother did the right thing for her. She speculates that her grandparents maintained the separation in an effort to provide her with the love and support that her mother could not offer during her childhood.

5

Ed

Ed, a dentist in practice with his brother and best friend, Richard, knew he was lucky. His life was wonderful and he was greatly fortified by his family and their love, support and generosity through the years.

One day Ed met "the most beautiful woman, the woman of my dreams." Ronda and Ed dated for 14 years; they were inseparable. They became each other's reason for living, and married in November, 2003.

Ronda died of breast cancer less than four months later.

The disease had been diagnosed in 2002, and Ed's career, life, and family were put on hold for two years as he and Ronda battled the enemy that waged war against her body. Ed was extremely fortunate to have people in his life who gave of their time to help. His brother took the helm of their business and his entire family lent support. Ed stayed with Ronda during her treatments and has no regrets.

Ed feels truly blessed to know God's precious love. He believes that his pain and suffering would have been debilitating were it not for his faith in God. He and Ronda listened to the Lord and He enabled them to get through otherwise insurmountable trials. Ed said, "Without Christ Jesus in my life, and without my family who have literally carried me, walking every step of the way with me, I couldn't have made it." Ed's advice? Become a faithful servant to your Lord and your spouse. Lastly, stand on the promises that were offered to you by God. As far as Ed is concerned, that is the only way.

6

Susan

Susan is proud to be unconventional. A cardiac nurse in a rehabilitation center, she is afforded the ability to administer healing in a holistic manner. Outside the rehabilitation setting, she is a holistic healthcare consultant, educator and hands-on practitioner.

Susan's beliefs were put to the test when her husband left her. The feelings of abandonment led her to places inside herself that she had never experienced. She suffered from insomnia, anxiety, deep grief and isolated bouts of depression. Susan likes to quote country singer Gary Allan, who said, "Life ain't always beautiful, sometimes it's just plain hard..." Believing that everything happens for a reason, and recognizing that life is dynamic and constantly shifting helped Susan wade through the muck.

As a woman of great faith, Susan believes that the power of positive thinking coupled with prayers of gratitude bring her the things she needs. She points out that attitude is an outgrowth of intention and what's in a person's heart and suggests that people regularly monitor their intention.

Susan displays an abundance of positive energy and is very kind to others. She believes that we are, first and foremost, spiritual beings whose nature is to seek homeostasis, a state of physical, emotional, mental and spiritual balance, and that we must consciously persevere to evolve and grow.

7

Cooper

They were the classic symptoms: weight loss, excessive thirst and increased urination. But it couldn't be. Cooper was only two years old. His mother, Melisa, had experienced a perfect pregnancy and had done everything right, so how could this be happening? But there it was, a diagnosis of juvenile diabetes.

Cooper's family rallied, adjusting their diet to reflect the restrictions that were placed on Cooper. Following the example of Cooper's father, Scott, the family adopted an attitude of gratitude. Scott pointed out that the diagnosis could have been much worse. Cooper might have been diagnosed with a more serious, or even a terminal illness. They might have left the hospital with no child at all.

Melisa's advice to parents who have children with diabetes or any other manageable disease is to be confident and encouraging. Melisa believes in the trickle-down effect, saying, "How will your child feel about himself if you don't have a positive attitude? After all, the child is not his diagnosis."

Melisa and her husband have always encouraged Cooper and have never made him feel different from other children. With parents like Melisa and Scott, how could he be anything other than buoyant and determined?

With a smile on her face, this mother walks her talk. Her pain is the same as any other parent hurting for a child; it is her attitude that separates her from parents who are negative and despondent.

Melisa's parents are partners in Cooper's care and they share her views. They believe that not hovering or worrying constantly about Cooper's health has produced a healthy, well-adjusted child. Cooper is energetic and athletic—a fun little boy who doesn't act spoiled or special, even though his parents would tell you that he *is* special.

8

Jeanne

Jeanne was a woman in charge. Physically compact and efficient, Jeanne plunged through life. She was usually awake, with a multitude of items crossed off her to-do list before the sun came up.

Jeanne had just finished a major project at work and was ready to tackle the next one when the world as she knew it was pulled out from under her feet. When Jeanne left work that fateful day, she was feeling accomplished. Little did she know, she would not walk back through that door for six months.

At home that evening, she found herself coughing persistently. She had been fighting a bad cold for weeks. During one violent coughing attack, Jeanne heard a whooshing noise in her ear and became very dizzy. Her entire body tightened. Her husband called

911 while checking her soaring blood pressure. Jeanne had had an aneurism and went into surgery with a mere 20 percent chance of survival. She doesn't recall the hours immediately following the surgery. However, she had plenty of opportunity to reflect during her one month hospitalization. This health crisis was the pivotal event that began a process of major change in Jeanne's life.

In typical Jeanne fashion, during the cognizant part of her recovery she maintained a survivor mentality. She thought,

"I am going to make it. I will survive." While in rehabilitation, her therapist told her she was walking faster than he was. Finally Jeanne was discharged from the hospital.

After six months, Jeanne returned to work sporting a new attitude. She had been forced to appreciate the art of balance. Accustomed to walking the precarious line between home, work, and family, she learned to make time for another person who was crucial to the equation—herself. She made a clear and conscience decision to take care of herself. Jeanne deeply appreciates life. She strives to keep that balance and stay true to the attitude that has helped her heal.

9

David

David earned a Ph.D. in clinical psychology and has been practicing for about 35 years. He is exuberant and engaging. You can not help being drawn to his passion. He has the unique ability to make you feel that you are the only person in the world and that what you are saying is of utmost importance. His patients profess that his nontraditional, yet professional style is very healing. David does not like to see other people suffering, and is driven to help them find solutions.

His practice was flourishing and all was well with David and his wife, Janet. Then challenging events started to happen. First, David parted with his best friend and business partner, with whom he no longer saw eye-to-eye. Then David lost a major contract. With managed care a major factor, the success of his practice dropped significantly. While still trying to adjust to these difficulties, he was notified that his practice owed $60,000 in back taxes, the result of an honest error. This was the proverbial "final straw."

While Janet tried to offer comfort, at home David became reclusive.

During one of his darkest moments, a "light" went off inside David's head. All his life he had been a dreamer. Now he summoned that quality from deep within. He phoned his wife from the steps of a courthouse where he had just testified as an expert witness and said, "I'm back." For the first time in months, David sensed his core strength.

When David counsels others who are experiencing similar business dilemmas, he advises them to hold on to their dreams, focus on their unique strengths and never let go. He urges clients to visualize their goals and relish their accomplishments, even when life's hurdles seem insurmountable.

David has stopped the self-criticism and self-condemnation. He now embraces his self-worth. After all, he did survive and now thrives. Seven investors were the silver lining to David's black cloud. They believed in him and his commitment to others. David says that good people will come forward to help and urges that we trust those people and be willing to ask for and accept help.

Today, one David's greatest passions is sharing with others the power of self-awareness in personal and business life as he encourages them to be heroes in their own special ways.

10

Gary

It was November of 2003 and Gary had decided to clean all the fallen leaves out of the gutters one more time before extremely cold weather settled in. The ladder fell and Gary suffered a traumatic brain injury. After being hospitalized for a period of time, he was

sent home to recover. Once home, Gary suffered a seizure, which resulted from an undiscovered aneurysm. Emergency surgery was performed, but Gary slipped into a coma and the future looked bleak.

When Gary regained consciousness, he faced many obstacles. He could neither see nor walk properly. He could not swallow, so for a number of weeks food was supplied directly to his stomach. A long road to recovery lay ahead.

Gary's family was supportive. His youngest son, a college junior, stayed home from school for a semester to help his dad.

(He has now graduated and taken a job close by his parents.) After graduating from law school, Gary's oldest son returned home to live for two years. Gary's wife supported Gary both emotionally and physically. She expressed her love and respect by keeping Gary on track. The relationship had always been close, but Gary's recovery gave it a new dimension.

The one thing that made Gary feel better about himself and probably expedited his healing was golf—his passion. A naturally competitive person who enjoys the camaraderie that comes with play, Gary reports that golf gave him confidence and made him feel normal. Gary needed months of physical therapy to regain his ability to grip the club and hit the ball. His former junior high school football coach guided him through workouts several days a week. Gary told me, "You always want to please your coach. I'm still that way."

Gary traveled to Chicago where he received outpatient therapy for eight hours a day. More coaching from the rehabilitation staff accelerated his recovery, as did the emotional fuel he received from a longtime friend who accompanied him on the journey.

11

Beth

In 2005, Beth started having excruciating headaches. Their magnitude was so great, they made her nauseous and caused her to double over with pain. Not very opportune when planning your 13-year-old child's birthday party. At the persistent urging of a friend, Beth reluctantly went to the hospital. Once admitted, she was treated with a drug that caused her to suffer a major reaction and slip into a coma. Beth's husband, Norman, made arrangements for a helicopter to airlift Beth to the medical facility at the University of Virginia in Charlottesville. The helicopter was forced to turn back because of intense fog, but ultimately made it.

While at the University, Beth came out of the coma, and everyone's spirits lifted. However, that elation was soon dashed when Beth suffered a series of strokes and required a brain biopsy.

The ordeal was devastating to Beth, who had three children at home almost 300 miles away.

The entire experience was also humbling. Beth was accustomed to being in charge. She was the person who ran the carpools, planned the parties, and took care of everything in a seamless manner. An avid gardener, Beth's gardening "therapy" had to be put on hold for her medical therapy—not quite as relaxing. She was in a hospital bed, far from her home and children, with an uncertain future.

In the wake of the experience, Beth has a fresh appreciation for her husband. His love, support and vision have given her renewed faith in her marriage. She explains, "Norm was with me the entire time. He was kind and tender in caring for me. I was more exposed and vulnerable than at any time in my life. I had to surrender, first to God and then to Norm."

Beth draws parallels between human love and God's almighty love. She feels that the love reflected in Norm's eyes has given her a tangible glimpse of the way God loves us. Beth's message to others is to surrender prior to illness—to give up control instead of trying to sit in the driver's seat of life. Instead of being "manager of the universe," Beth advises friends to manage nothing more than their own lives and troubles, which are far less consuming.

Tami, Deb and Beth

Today, Beth is lighthearted and in the moment, with good humor and an awesome attitude. To her, attitude is everything.

12

Max

Max came into the world in December, 2000. Born a robust eight pounds with a normal Apgar score (measuring pulse, breathing, activity, reflexes and coloration), he appeared the picture of health. His mother wanted to believe this was true; however, her experience as the mother of three told her otherwise. Her concern grew with Max's refusal to nurse and an insidious failure to thrive. Still, at repeated medical visits, Max's parents were told that nothing was wrong.

When Max was 10 days old, additional blood work was completed and again pronounced normal. However, the physician said that the parents should take Max to the emergency room the next day if he continued to refuse both water and milk.

The next morning at 4 a.m., after a full night of no feeding, the decision was made. At the hospital, a spinal tap was performed to rule out meningitis. While that test was negative, additional blood work revealed a potassium level that one doctor labeled "inconsistent with life." Max was admitted to the Neonatal Intensive Care Unit, and a flurry of activity with endocrinologists, cardiologists, and other specialists followed.

Although the prognosis was uncertain, Max's mother realized that the family could control how they faced the situation. A sense of calm prevailed, and the parents believed that no matter what happened, Max would be fine. This attitude was necessary not only for Max, but for three older siblings whose lives continued outside the walls of the hospital.

At some point during this hospital hell, the rare disorder Congenital Adrenal Hyperplasia (CAH) was mentioned as the possible culprit. Nurses told the parents that many CAH babies born to inexperienced mothers died because their symptoms went unrecognized. According to the nurses, CAH mortality was also higher in states that did not screen newborns for the disorder, a situation that has since been remedied.

When a final diagnosis of CAH was made, Max was moved to a regular room. The move coincided with a fireworks display to celebrate the New Year. And what a celebration it was for the family! With little Max out of danger, the family felt a genuine appreciation for the truly important things in life.

Max is now a healthy, vibrant five year old. He takes medication three times a day and will for the rest of his life. No one who knows Max can imagine life without him. This sweet and super-charged dynamo has one particularly important thing going for him: dedicated, loyal parents who do not accept easy answers. Parents with an attitude of gratitude.

13

Suzanne

Tumultuous was an accurate description of Suzanne's life. Soon after she moved to West Virginia with her two young daughters, she and her husband divorced. After working hard for a brief period, she decided to go to law school. It was a struggle to keep up with her studies while caring for the children, but she managed. Then, after completing her first year of law school, Suzanne married George, without whose companionship her life would be incomplete and empty.

During her final year of law school, Suzanne began to feel extremely tired. The first medical diagnosis was exhaustion. However, after moving back to Charleston, Suzanne, then 40, learned that she had multiple sclerosis (MS).

Suzanne has always had an admirable attitude and is not one to sit around feeling sorry for herself. She speculates that, had she not met this medical fate, relationships she held dear might not have been as sweet and fulfilling. Suzanne used to fear that she would embarrass her young daughters by having to depend on their assistance to maneuver, but they, along with George, quickly alleviated that fear with their respect and devotion.

Suzanne points out that having a frustrating disease with many uncontrollable symptoms and complications has produced some remarkable benefits, such as when a couple of young, handsome college students approached her at a game and offered their assistance. Suzanne embraces rather than refuses offers of help, which is another wonderful attribute. She has never been angry about her fate, believes in a higher power and does not worry about the future. "Whatever is coming is coming and I refuse to let it interfere with today," she says.

14

Jason

Jason's young world was rocked when he learned of his father's diagnosis. It was a death sentence: Stage 4 melanoma. His father would soon die, and Jason and his twin brother, Jeff, were only 11 years old.

Two years later, at 13, Jason was without a father. Soon he was without a mother as well. She was diagnosed with a terminal illness shortly after his father died and succumbed when Jason was 18.

For a brief period, Jason turned to partying to soothe his pain. However, he quickly came to his senses and realized that this was not the life his parents would have wanted for him. They would have wanted him to savor the seasons of his life.

Miraculously, Jason pulled himself up by his bootstraps and went to college. Immersion in academics and campus life allowed him to block out his tumultuous teens and he matured seemingly overnight, turning the negatives of his earlier years into positives.

Today, Jason is happily married and feels that his previous losses have allowed him to savor his relationship with his wife more than he otherwise might have. At this writing, the couple are expecting a child. Jason is elated and focused on becoming the kind of father that he enjoyed having for such a brief period of time. He still abides by his father's advice and wisdom, which are always with him. Jason believes that many life lessons were instilled through the care and devotion of his parents. They taught the virtue of hard work and moral values. Jason attends church regularly because that was always important in his family.

Jason says, "When I talk about attitude, I mean that I don't think negatively, but always try to look on the bright side of life, savoring every happy moment. I want to make sure that I teach my children the same moral values, self discipline, and belief systems that were imparted to me. I want to make them aware that life is a precious gift and every day should be unwrapped anew and approached with a fresh attitude."

15

Marti

The diagnosis was a benign acoustic neuroma on the right side of her brain. She was only 28 years old and had been suffering from headaches, nausea, and dizziness. Two separate surgeries to remove the tumor were performed at University Hospital in Pittsburgh. Each one was long and tedious. The tumor was successfully removed, but the right side of her face was left paralyzed, and she had no hearing in her right ear. A third surgery was performed to remedy those problems, with minimal success.

Marti's friends were all crushed. She was and still is a beautiful woman, as pretty inside as out. Her ordeal was traumatic to everyone, but especially to her family, who were devastated by her changed appearance. However, Marti had the fortitude to accept her condition and get out in the world, and because of that courage found the love of her life.

Marti met her husband, Mike, two years after the surgeries. She was thrilled that he thought she was beautiful. They were

married in 1986 and began a series of moves that were unsettling for her, because each one further separated Marti from her large West Virginia family. The youngest of eight children, Marti was close to her parents and siblings, so the distance that separated them was difficult. A bright spot in Marti's life was the birth of her daughter, Sarah.

More sadness ensued. Marti's father died and, not long afterwards, Mike died from a massive heart attack. Marti moved back to West Virginia to be close to her family. Mike's sudden and untimely death devastated her. Sarah was five years old when they moved in with Marti's aging mother. A short while later, Marti's mother fell, injuring her hip. She died during the surgery to repair it. Marti had suffered more than her share of grief.

Marti credits her survival to the love of family and friends, and to her determination to be there for her 17-year-old daughter. At first she was angry at God when these traumatic events occurred, but then she concluded that God only takes the best. Even though Marti's and Mike's time together was short, the marriage gave her Sarah. When Marti looks at Sarah, she sees Mike. Marti's advice to anyone facing difficult obstacles in life is to turn to God, family and friends.

16

Stefanie

It was the best year of Stefanie's life. She was 25 years old, had landed a great job and was married to the love of her life. The newlyweds had purchased a small, quaint home and were settling

into married life. Then, on a Monday afternoon, one phone call changed everything.

Stefanie had the day off and was in the kitchen when a manager at her husband's office phoned with the news that her husband had been in a terrible accident. She needed to get to the hospital immediately. Stefanie felt a heaviness in her chest and the blood seemed to drain from her body. When she arrived at the hospital, she learned that her husband had died. That morning's goodbye kiss had been their last.

After the funeral, Stefanie felt lost, lonely and dead inside. For days, all she could do was cry. She sometimes drove alone on the freeway hoping that some big truck would put her out of her misery.

Stefanie grieved for several months while holding tight to her Christian faith. Eventually she found peace in the belief that her husband was in a better place. She prayed to God daily for strength, guidance and direction. Those who knew Stefanie at the time testified to her beautiful smile and abundant energy. She exuded a sweet effervescence. Although she was lost and hurting inside, Stefanie continued her life and made the most of each passing day. She never wanted sympathy.

After six years, Stefanie remarried. At this writing, she and her new husband are expecting their first child. Stefanie is grateful for God's many blessings and believes that all things happen for a reason, although sometimes we don't understand what it is. The tragedy of her first husband's death taught Stefanie that life is short and each day must be lived as if it were the last. " Treat people the way you want to be treated, because you never know when their time on earth will end. Never go to bed or leave for work while angry at your spouse."

17

Steve

Steve was enjoying life. He and his beautiful wife, Dawn, had all the things they had ever wanted, including a brand new home and three-year-old twin boys.

One day, when Steve and Dawn were at a football game with friends, one of the women confided that she had breast cancer. On their way home, Dawn told Steve that she thought she might have breast cancer, too. Although Dawn was scheduled to

have a mammogram in three months, she and Steve went to the doctor immediately. Their worst fears were confirmed. Steve felt weak and helpless at the news. It seemed impossible for this to be happening.

Dawn's rock-solid attitude carried them through months of treatment. Steve remembers that when Dawn went to her first chemotherapy session she started rearranging the room. She told the nurses that she would organize a fundraiser and urged them to put flowers on the tables and pictures on the walls. There she was in the throes of cancer, redecorating the unit. "She is a phenomenal woman who taught me the value of a positive outlook as she went through her trials and suffering," Steve said admiringly.

Other than Dawn and his sons, Steve's most valuable companion throughout this time was his faith. Steve grew up in a Christian home with a loving family. Dawn's experience with cancer taught him that we have a tenuous hold on life, but that a higher power carries us when we are unable to think and act clearly.

18

Lois

Lois was at the school where she teaches when she first felt the lump in her breast. She put her hand on her heart and waited. There was nothing she could say to her husband, Gary, that wouldn't upset him. A coach, Gary's high school basketball team was vying for the championship that day, and Lois didn't want to distract him.

She felt the mass again in the shower several nights later and telephoned her doctor the next day. She was scheduled for a mammogram in one month, but the doctor insisted that she be seen that very day.

The suspicious mass was jagged and difficult to manipulate. It had to be removed. Lois chose a surgeon and placed a call to his office for an appointment. When she arrived home, Gary was waiting for her on the front steps. "Why are you seeing Dr. Foster on Monday?" was his urgent question. Lois explained the worrisome news.

The growth was removed by means of a lumpectomy and Lois was thrilled to learn that the cancer had not invaded her lymph nodes. The family celebrated. However, more crushing news followed. Ultimately, Lois underwent two separate mastectomies, followed by chemotherapy and reconstructive surgery. As it turned out, Lois' rehabilitation came at a good time. She was able to get to know and care for her infant grandson while his parents were at their respective jobs.

Lois has never looked back. She nurtures an attitude of gratitude and has happily returned to her regular schedule. Teaching has allowed her to regain a sense of normalcy. Lois offers this advice: do not give up at the moment of diagnosis when everything seems bleak. Stand up and fight. Think about surviving. Don't relinquish the opportunity to win the war being waged against your body. Never say no to survival.

According to Lois, what doesn't kill you will make you stronger.

19

Theresa

Theresa's first husband, David, was murdered when Theresa was 26 years old. It was 1979 and they had been married four years. He was an Amtrak agent in Charleston, West Virginia. He was working in his office when three intruders jumped the counter and shot him in the head. They had made an earlier futile attempt to rob the Virginian Theatre and the Amtrak office was their next target. Theresa lamented, "Your entire future is planned and suddenly everything goes black."

That was 27 years ago, but the memories are still fresh. Theresa remembers getting dressed for the funeral, and she remembers the flowers—103 baskets of them. She was overwhelmed by the number of people who reached out to her. The criminal trials followed, and she had to deal with all the attention they garnered.

Theresa went on with her career and worked diligently to recover from the pain of losing her husband. She was finally able to surrender her anger, not because the hurt was gone, but because she had to keep going. Many people rallied around Theresa and she became stronger with each passing year.

Life got better. When Theresa was 29, Patrick came along. He was tall, dark and handsome, with a heart of gold. The sparks were immediate and are still evident today. Theresa says, "He was the angel that God sent to me." After 17 years of marriage, Theresa and Patrick adopted a Russian baby. Chance is now 7 years old and the apple of his parents' eyes. Looking back, Theresa says it was their destiny.

Theresa has always felt a great deal of compassion for others. Her friends and family say that she is too generous with her time. It appears that doing for others is not only gratifying, but takes her mind off herself. Says Theresa, "I believe God has a plan and that we are like little grains of sand being sifted around. He is the wind that blows us and carries us through."

20

Tom

It was every parent's nightmare—a knock at the door followed by devastating news: your child has been killed in an accident. That was the news that shattered Tom's world when he was told that his son, Chris, a college freshman, was dead.

Chris had gone out for the evening. Sometimes Tom and Jane would hear their son arrive home and sometimes his reentry escaped their notice. Typical college student. They were disbelieving. Surely it was a mistake. Perhaps someone borrowed their son's car. Tom took a deep breath and placed the necessary telephone calls. The family was in shock.

Then Tom did what is expected of fathers—he went back to work. Burying himself in his career was like a salve. Rev. Smith, a longtime family friend and minister, had also experienced the loss of a child. He gave Tom permission to be angry. Rev. Smith said that the loss was not God's fault. Rather, God, having lost his own child, shared Tom's pain. He said that when God was angry the heavens trembled and shook, and the temple curtain tore completely when Jesus died.

Tom decided to look for the good in life and in that horrible event. Years later, his daughter, Jennifer, had a child on the anniversary of her brother's death and named the baby after Chris. The birth of the child was healing.

Tom likens the loss of a child to major surgery. You heal, but you always carry a scar. Tom's scar is sensitive and visible, even after the healing. He attributes his survival to reading and frequently citing Rev. Smith's article, "Sit Down God, I am Angry!" Tom advises others to seek refuge in their own belief systems during trying times.

21

Jack

Jack is no stranger to pain and has always dealt with physical and mental anguish quietly and reclusively. The youngest of five children, Jack joined the Navy at a young age. He often reminisces about those days. A self-admitted alcoholic, Jack gave up the bottle when his youngest daughter was born. I am that daughter.

People describe Jack as a charming gentleman with a fabulous sense of humor, and as a man's man. Brave, and never afraid to defend the underdog, he is an individual with his own ideas. His interests in psychology and holistic medicine were ahead of their time. Our family often traveled, and to pass the time he led us in singing hymns. Those hymns are etched in my soul and provide my heart great refuge to this day.

Several years ago, while reading *The Wind is My Mother* by Bear Heart Williams, I was overcome with guilt for having blamed my father for the pain I experienced in childhood. I resented his having left the family and often imagined how different things would have been if he had stayed. Bear Heart's book could have been written by my dad. Like the author, Jack is Native American. I was riveted by the teachings in the book, which were very similar to my father's lessons. Bear Heart helped me find forgiveness in my heart. All my resentment, guilt, and blame dissipated.

Jack had numerous health problems. When he was in his forties, he experienced heart problems. Later he developed bladder and kidney cancer. He never complained and when asked how he felt would often reply, "If I were any better, there would be two of me," or "Great honey, just terrific." Even lying on his death bed in a physically diminished body, he still answers, "Terrific, much better, thank you."

I told Jack over a year ago that I was writing this book. His response was, "I am glad you didn't wait until I died and talk badly about me." What a brave and courageous demeanor he had during that interview. He told me, "Death is not bad or scary. I have had a good life and enjoyed forgiveness within my soul. I want nothing and would change nothing. Everything that happened made me stronger and defined who I am. If I could change one thing today, I would brighten the look on your sweet, loving face."

I will always love you, my dear and gentle Dad.